"*Brave Art* is a call to action to come home to your own heart. We need this kind of wisdom and encouragement now more than ever. Any writer or artist struggling with self-doubt and fear will be forever changed by this book."

– LAUREN SAPALA, author and writing coach

"*Brave Art* is for the artist, musician, inventor, writer, entrepreneur, and for all those called to create something new.

I don't consider myself artistic in the traditional sense, so when Mark asked if I would review his latest book, I wasn't expecting what happened next. Despite being deep in the throes of launching our first Miracle Café in Wales, I was captivated and devoured every word. This well-written and insightful work encouraged me through lonely times of self-doubt, and challenged me to dream big and take courage to create what is in my heart. So whatever the canvas of your calling, you can expect *Brave Art* to be a catalyst to uncover your hidden treasure and activate the creative within."

– ALISS CRESSWELL, author, and founder of Spirit Lifestyle & Miracle Cafés

"This is the book I needed twenty years ago, and I expect a well-thumbed copy will still be on my shelf twenty years from now. *Brave Art* is enough to draw the most stubborn creative person out of their shell. Mark does more than just encourage us to make pretty things, he calls us to a life of perpetual creativity."

– TIM GOUGH, author and award-winning leadership blogger

"*Brave Art* dares us to imagine what life might be like if we live to our greatest creative potential. And this message isn't just for artists in the narrow sense; it is for anyone who has felt the call of creativity.

Mark writes with compassion straight from the heart, and his incisive commentary and insight get to the root of why we so often feel put off our creative pursuits, and, more importantly, what to do about it. This book is both brave and artistic, which aptly demonstrates the kind of work it will inspire. Please read it."

– BEN TRIGG, multi-instrumentalist and songwriter

"If you, just like me, have had moments questioning the point of why you should be creating, Mark beautifully explains why you ought never stop. He inspires the kind of courage that will show the way to hope and unity through creativity, even in these times of such division. It is all about bravery; the bravery to step into who we are meant to be and to share our messages in ways unique to each one of us.

Having been deeply moved and guided by Mark's previous book, *The Creative Wound*, the theme of *Brave Art* feels like the natural next step on my creative journey."

– EMMA-KLARA SANDBERG, photographer and floral designer

"*Brave Art* is a strong yet gentle call to bring beauty into ugly places by bravely stepping forward, despite our uncertainty and fear. Mark reminds us of the difference between allowing ourselves to be caught up by what resonates with us, and getting caught up by distractions that separate us from ourselves and one another. It is a message of hope that we would do well to let settle and integrate into every part of our collective sense of being."

– ANDY MORT, songwriter and slow coach for gentle rebels

Brave Art

COURAGEOUS
CREATIVITY IN AN
AGE OF CONFORMITY

Mark Pierce

www.revelator.co.uk

Copyright

Copyright © 2022 Mark Pierce

All rights reserved. No part of this book may be reproduced in any form or by any electronic or mechanical means, including information storage and retrieval systems, without written permission from the author, except for the use of brief quotations.

Design & formatting: www.revelator.co.uk

Disclaimer: this book is not medical, mental health, or financial advice. It contains information and thoughts you may find helpful, but please seek personalised professional counsel if your situation needs it.

Contents

An Invitation	1
Ed	7
The Essence Of Art	9
This One Is Yours	17
Born In A Barn	19
Brave And Beautiful	29
The Nature Of Beauty	35
Proper Art Or Propaganda	45
Break The (Jelly) Mould	55
Soul Trader	61
Actively Still	65
There's Knowing And There's Knowing	71
Seeing Red, I Think	77
Stealing Seed	83
More Than An Echo	89
Rutting Stags	95
Loving And Letting Go	105

Just My Type	111
Creative, Sensitive & Misunderstood	117
Relationship	121
Remember When	131
Perfectly Safe	143
Two Tyred	151
9485 Days Later	155
Don't Die Of Exposure	161
Provision	165
The Full-Time Creative	173
Work To A Budget & Budget To Work	179
Embrace Restrictions	185
Inspiration	189
The Day Before Everything	197
Treasure The Questions	201
Our Working Worldview	209
Cracking The Chaos Code	211
Wetwang	215
The Commissioning	225
Please Leave A Review	229
Notes	231
Bibliography	239
About The Author	243
Acknowledgements	245
Excerpt From The Creative Wound	247

An Invitation

I know something about you.

You are creative.

Okay, I can hear the arguments already: "But you don't know *me*. I'm the exception that proves the rule. I've not got a creative bone in my body."

If this sounds like you, pause and pay careful attention to your thoughts.

As you craft your argument against my statement, you are mentally gathering pictures, words, feelings, memories, imaginations, and projections, as evidence. Then, you select the best parts and position them to have the most impact.

In effect, you are using creative thinking techniques to prove that you can't think creatively.

Ironic, isn't it?

You might as well accept it, you *are* creative – although perhaps you've forgotten how to be so, and especially how to be so on purpose.

Many adults believe only a select few are born with creative talent. They also tend to believe they're not one of the lucky ones to be apportioned any of it. However, in truth, creativity isn't the rare privilege of a gifted minority but is a learned skill, and one we all can develop.

Back in the late 1980s, I was the guitarist in a band and used to have a big, heavy rock hairstyle. It wasn't so much sleek, flowing locks as it was a privet hedge; its monumental proportions and flair for self-governance meant that whenever I stopped, my hair would keep going.

Can you picture that?

Good.

This is evidence enough to prove that you have what it takes to be creative, because creativity is rooted in your ability to imagine. The problem is, as we journey through life, we let ourselves be talked out of it.

And I want to talk us back into it.

So, I'm on a mission. A mission to wake up a generation of sleeping artists. A mission to stir the dormant talent in those of us born to create.

Which includes you.

Because you were born to create.

I'm convinced of this because creative ability is inherent in us all, it's just that not everybody knows it. Some once did, but have long since forgotten.

On reaching the lofty peaks of adulthood, many of us relegate imagination to being just kids' stuff, and go on to live as though our highest calling is compliance, not creativity. We never lose the ability, though, we just lock away our maker-of-interesting-things and try to forget.

But if you'll indulge me for a brief moment, and cast your mind back, do you remember as a child when you met *everything* with curiosity and imagination?

That is still you.

And no matter how inept you may feel right now, you are capable of far more than you realise. You have it in you to be an artist of one kind or another.

Of course, not everybody aspires to be an 'arty type'. You may never want to be a painter, writer, or musician, and that's okay because creativity applies to not only the arts, but to the whole of life. You'd expect artists to be creative, of course, but creativity is not the exclusive domain of those who paint, write, or play an instrument. It is a treasure hidden within every human heart and it yearns to be unearthed from the moment we take our first breath.

And we depend on its manifestation in so many ways.

It is my belief that a creative spirit, a curious mind, and a heart after beauty hold the answers to many of the serious problems we face today.

Whether you want to start your own business, write a song, innovate at work, or see the world through new eyes, producing anything that is meaningful, lasting, and significant demands a continual flow of creative ideas.

Although, that said, they are only part of the story.

Beyond creative ideas, you must be brave.

It takes bravery to try something new.

It takes bravery to revive something old.

It takes bravery to share your ideas.

It takes bravery to show your work.

It takes bravery to admit that you experience doubt.

It takes bravery to overcome fear.

It takes bravery to be vulnerable.

It takes bravery to say what needs to be said.

It takes bravery to be the only one standing.

It takes bravery to build when everyone else is tearing down.

It takes bravery to create.

It takes bravery to confront difficulty, uncertainty, pain,

intimidation, and even danger. But given enough time, your courage can become immovable, and eventually release you to produce your truest work: the work of an artist.

It's the artist who expresses the impact of life on the human heart. It's the artist who ignites fresh hope in the weary. It's the artist who offers beauty for ashes. And it's the brave artist who does this with love, and without apology.

Does this sound like you? Or who you want to be? Perhaps who you were born to be?

If so, consider this an invitation to take your place in the emerging creative revolution.

This is your call to renewed innocence and wonder, to have more questions than answers, but through those questions discover better answers.

This is your call to experiment, explore, and uncover hidden treasure, to embrace mystery and uncertainty with enthusiasm, and discover what might be possible beyond all that you currently know.

This is your call to help shape the world that is shaping us. So treat this book as a guided tour of the creative mind's luminous pathways and darkened alleys, and as a reminder of our indispensable need for imagination and beauty.

This is your call to brave art.

Ed

I met Ed at a creativity workshop I was delivering. A warm, unassuming character, he had travelled over an hour to join us in a cosy coffee shop buried in the back streets of a small Welsh coastal town.

The first exercise I assigned everyone that night was to draw a coffee cup. Most drew simple but adequate line drawings, but Ed's was dimensional, balanced, and showed a masterful grasp of light and shade. Evidently he was a seasoned artist.

And terminally ill with cancer.

He told me, "In years gone by I would have expressed my emotions in painting or music but, at a time when I really needed to, I had forgotten how."

He went on to share that, after reading my book *The Creative Wound* cover-to-cover twice in two days, he was rediscovering belief in himself and that his artistic desire was returning. The last I heard, he was learning the guitar and had started a creative writing degree.

Who starts a three-year course not knowing they'll be alive long enough to finish it?

Brave artists do.

Like Ed.

Never underestimate the catalytic potential of your creative life and the courage it can inspire in others. You may never reach The New York Times Best Seller list, Tate Modern, or whatever your equivalent is. You might instead do something greater, like helping to renew a fellow human being's hope. You might remind them why they should never stop creating. Which is what meeting Ed did for me.

Even if we never cross paths again, I will not forget him or his remarkable attitude.

As I gathered up the pens and pads at the end of the night, I came across the coffee cup sketch Ed had done. He'd left it behind.

I'm keeping it.

The Essence Of Art

What does blue look like?

You could talk for an hour and I still might not understand. But point to a cloudless summer sky and immediately I get it. Some things are easier to demonstrate than explain.

Can you describe the wind?

If you're like me, you will find it easier to explain what the wind does than what it is, and for most of us, that's what counts. Ultimately, though, the best method surpasses words altogether: you simply open the door and step outside. If you stand in a gale, you will feel it. And by leaning into the experience, you will have an irrefutable personal encounter. Experience always trumps theory.

Art is much the same way: describing its essence can be trickier than describing its effects. And as discussing creativity's effects is infinitely more edifying than bickering over theory, I urge you to seek out your own experiences, and wholly embrace the creative works that you find exciting.

In light of this, I encourage you to look up the references I make throughout this book wherever you can, be they paintings, pieces of music, or people. Stop reading and go look them up. I'll wait for you. Do this and you will enrich both yourself and your reading experience.

Definitions and parameters are impossible to avoid entirely, of course, but those I use are mainly as commentary on aspects of the whole. They're facets worth drawing your attention to rather than rules to be learned by rote.

Although they are related concepts, *creativity* and *art* are not directly interchangeable terms, and the wrangle over their definitions has raged for centuries. This highlights how significant they are to humanity. And also how elusive. They stubbornly refuse to be pinned down and are more alive and malleable than to let themselves be restricted to one shape or singular understanding.

No doubt you have seen a rainbow. If I asked you to draw one, you'd likely produce a striped arc with seven distinct solid colours. Most people have a similarly strong idea that this is what a rainbow should look like. But despite this popular view, a rainbow has no demarcation lines between each colour, because it is, in reality, a spectrum. So despite you being able to pick out distinct red, orange, yellow, green, blue, indigo, and violet hues, you will also find it impossible to pinpoint exactly where one colour transitions to the next.

We encounter the same kind of problem when trying to define creativity, art, craft, imagination, invention, ingenuity, and other related concepts, with any degree of accuracy. The lines often seem blurry and indefinite, with one concept sneakily merging into the next without us noticing.

So I aim to tread carefully and avoid giving art and creativity dogmatic definitions. Discoveries continue to be made, and our aspect broadens accordingly, which, when talking about creativity, is just as it should be.

However, as starting points for us to work from, I offer you my simple descriptions: creativity solves a problem, and art makes it beautiful.

For instance, whenever I'm hungry, I hunt around the kitchen and throw together some food between two slices of bread to make myself a sandwich. In short, I solve my problem (hunger) using creativity (finding and combining ingredients). But my friend Paul would solve this problem in an entirely different way, and his solution would not only be creative but artistic. You see, Paul is a chef and has culinary skills way beyond mine, so the sandwich he'd make would be far tastier. He would probably even bake the bread himself.

Paul and I could both solve the same problem, and each of us would do it by creating something. But Paul would make it beautiful.

If you apply creativity, artistry, and a love for beauty into everything you do, making a sandwich can be as emotionally fulfilling as painting a masterpiece. How much better would life be if you and I were able to live and create from such a full heart every day. If you limit the use of your creative talents to your spare time, you'll atrophy and be miserable.

Today you may not paint your answer to the Mona Lisa, but you might make a sandwich that transforms someone's lunchtime. And that still counts, because not all creativity is art in the traditional classical sense. 'Nonarty' people can be immensely creative, which is good news if you don't fancy becoming a painter, author, or composer.

My friend Andy Mort, musician, writer, and host of *The Gentle Rebel Podcast*, describes creativity this way: "To bring something into the world that wouldn't exist in the way it does without your presence in the process of its becoming."

The key word here is presence. Our active presence brings new things into the world.

We create homes, families, connections, communities, and belonging. We create spaces and safe places. We create meals, moments, and memories. We create possibilities and opportunities. Together we created the past and together we will create the future, one in which creative thought shall be central. And if we are to thrive in the days ahead, more than ever we must maintain our ability to dream.

Without exception, whatever your area of interest happens to be, things go better when you've cultivated the ability to dream and the courage to do. When you are convinced about your ability to generate new ideas, and have the tenacity to carry them out, you are well equipped. And as life itself is the most exquisite art form we will ever grapple with, is not every moment deserving of our grandest dreams and best creative endeavours?

As computers and robots take the weight of repetitive work, we are heading into an ideas economy where the currency is imagination. So we must allow ourselves to be ever more curious and inventive. But herein lies our problem: since the early 1990s we have been enduring something of a creativity crisis. Studies by one of the world's leading creativity researchers, Dr Kyung-Hee Kim, Professor of Creativity and Innovation at the College of William & Mary, have revealed an alarming decline in creativity. While IQ has been on an upward trajectory, our collective ability to think creatively has been plummeting.[1]

As a creative professional for over a quarter of a century, this trend troubles me. And as a dad, it troubles me enough to do something about. It's vital we retain our imagination, cultivate it, and reverse this disturbing decline.

And so we need artists and creators to step up. We need them to throw ice water over the heads of the sleeping so that they open their eyes and relearn how to see. This ability to stir people is why the creative mind is dangerous to those who oppose freedom, and why you'll need courage if you're going to interpret and express truth and beauty as you see it.

Art helps us process our lives and bear truthful witness to what we've seen and experienced. It offers beauty when things are ugly. Through art, we clarify how we perceive and relate to the world. Words, images, and sounds resonate within us to create emotions, and these help us articulate our thoughts and feelings in ways we couldn't manage on our own. We desperately need more creators of these works – these makers of moments – if we are to decipher some kind of meaning from the suffering and confusion we all witness. This is why we call upon artists to share their perspective and interpretation, because, in so doing, they hold open a space for us to form our own.

Art, including the art you make, is a portal to an epiphany, a doorway to the sublime. It carries with it revelation; and the truest art, in all its forms, often reveals its secrets progressively: great stories continue to speak new and profound things even after the hundredth telling; a song may accompany a person's lifetime and never grow dull; and there are paintings that hang for centuries and never fail to transport the viewer, generation upon generation.

These works engulf us within something transcendent and eternal. They are a place to immerse ourselves and emerge with a better understanding of who we are. As Thomas Merton once noted, "Art enables us to find ourselves and lose ourselves at the same time."[2]

Regrettably, though, art cannot manufacture meaning where it did not already exist, and thus it cannot alleviate us of a meaningless existence. But it can reacquaint us with the essential beauty we've turned away from and reveal what has been with us all along, hidden in plain sight, veiled in shadow.

A turn of phrase in a book, a chord change in a piece of music, a flavour, a photograph, each has the power to evoke specific feelings, or connect us back to ones that were previously out of reach. I'm thankful for these moments, and through my work I hope to make similar experiences possible for others.

Our love of aesthetics and meaning is intrinsic to the human experience and distinguishes us from other living creatures. Writer and award-winning filmmaker J. F. Martel says, "In the creative imagination, things are revealed to humans that are hidden from the rest of the known cosmos."[3] And Dr John Medina, an expert in the genetics of human brain development, says in his book

Brain Rules, "Symbolic reasoning separates us from animals."[4]

Animals live by instinct, and while we too are instinctual in many ways, we also plan and create. We imagine, innovate, design, and beautify. We tell stories to explain the world and to bring comfort to one another. We dream of making things better and collaborate in using the resources and abilities we have to produce new, beautiful, and valuable things.

You are made for more than carrying out directives. You've been created to create.

This One Is Yours

An express train roars through a small countryside station, shuttling people from one metropolis to the next. It is impossible to board, too fast, too dangerous.

Suited figures blur past, speeding by to broker their power deals. No one thinks to make time or room for you – you're too small-fry and, besides, you're waiting in entirely the wrong place. Anyway, even if you could climb aboard, your choice of destination would be no choice at all. And once you're on, you're stuck. There is no getting off until you arrive where you're being taken.

So you stand alone on the tiny platform, feeling more trainspotter than adventurer as you watch the locomotive barrelling down the line and out of eyeshot. Then you turn, preparing to make your own way.

Yours is not the common route. There are no pre-paid tickets or pre-laid tracks to where you're headed. A wayfarer you may be, but there is autonomy in your wandering. You're not lost, you're free. Although if you are to cut this path, you must act now because there will soon be no more time. Your window will close.

So spend not a second more wondering at another's adventure.

This one is yours.

Born In A Barn

What is the most stressful thing you can do?

Changing career, moving house, getting divorced, losing friends, starting a business, physical pain or discomfort, money pressures, loneliness and isolation? There is quite a list of possibilities.

Here's my top tip: as far as it depends on you, don't ever try them all at once.

I'll spare you the sordid details, but during a calamitous couple of years, most of what I considered certain in my life collapsed. While still adjusting to life as a freelancer after years of design agency employment, my first marriage ended, taking the house with it. Then relationships went south in a faith community I'd long been a member of, and I ended up parting ways with them too.

Just about every place or relationship I belonged to evaporated in a brief moment of time: social, personal, professional – all gone, leaving me bewildered and bereft.

Life had led me to a precipice, and I'd reached an all-or-nothing moment. A tipping point, if you will.

Faced with this kind of reality, you either play the victim or set your face like flint and determine you're going to get through it and not be crushed. You unswervingly decide that you are going to grow. Even if you legitimately *are* a victim, don't *play* the victim. In most stories, the victim role is a small one, and you alone decide if you're going to play a small role in the story of your own life.

Without a doubt, this was a devastating period for me. But it was also a clean slate. A second chance I never saw coming or realised I needed.

So I started to dream about what I could create from this nightmare.

I'd been recording and producing my own music for years and helping friends with theirs, but had done nothing on a professional basis. I paid the bills as a graphic designer and photographer, which somehow seemed like the 'proper' work that music production couldn't be for me.

Why not, though? Could I pursue my love for writing, arranging, recording, and producing music, and find a way to build it more fundamentally into my life, including as a means of income?

Could I respect myself if I didn't even give it a shot?

I realised that to have a chance, I would have to flip everything and radically disrupt myself – as if life wasn't disrupted enough already.

Wherever I've lived, I've always designated a small area for my freelance work. But if I was going to record music, I needed much more space – not just a spare room in a house. And because living and working in the same place is usually the most cost-effective, instead of looking for somewhere to live that had a small space to work from, I started looking for a big space to work from that I could also live in.

So when I came across a converted barn in the country on the outskirts of York, I knew I'd found the place. The main room had high ceilings and charming beams that gave it the perfect inspirational vibe for recording music.

I wouldn't entertain the idea of working from a room that was a charmless modern box, and I fell in love with that big space for its potential as a studio. But to say the decor of the living quarters was rudimentary is doing it a kindness. The upside of that, though, was being able to negotiate an affordable rent for such a large studio space.

And so it transpired that I left a small, comfortable, modern house to set up camp in a big, cold barn. The living area was cramped and the overall less-than-palatial experience was akin to camping indoors. But, at times as a child, I'd lived in a household with no heating, no bathroom, and no running hot water, so I knew I could 'rough it' a while for the sake of my growth and creative progress. In many ways, the rudimentary nature of the place helped me to focus on what mattered most at the time – sharpening my skills, finding clients, and creating music. And as I was no longer in a relationship, and no one was depending on me, I had the opportunity to invest heavily in my craft and my future.

The creative life isn't just about making that final piece of work or acknowledging your raw potential. Much more hangs on how resourceful and inventive you are in making your work a possibility in the first place. Sometimes you need imagination to even reach the starting line.

A few weeks after moving into the barn, I'd built a new website and put it live. I'd also spread the word via my muso friends, and distributed flyers to local music shops.

Now all I could do was wait and hope for an enquiry to come flooding in.

Weeks passed. Nothing. I wondered if I'd made a terrible mistake.

Then one day, in February 2010, an email arrived that changed everything. A few days later, songwriter Maggie Adams and her husband Hugh turned up at the door of my new studio.

Over the years, I've met hundreds of new people in hundreds of meetings, but this time I was nervous. It mattered. This was my first proper recording studio enquiry. And I felt like a fraud.

On top of that, heating the big room on a freezing winter night was expensive. I hoped they didn't stay long.

They stayed long.

And I'm so glad they did.

Poor old Hugh had the job of lugging Maggie's big, heavy Yamaha keyboard workstation across the stone courtyard and into the studio. I like to think I helped him with it, but I probably just made him a cup of tea.

As the couple squashed themselves onto my comedically small sofa, I guessed they were somewhere in their fifties. Both were instantly likeable, an impression that wasn't harmed any by their affable Scottish lilt.

Maggie had never worked with a recording studio before and was understandably nervous about asking a stranger for feedback on her songs. These were her babies.

I later found out she'd been so anxious about it she'd been physically ill before setting off to meet me.

As we listened to the songs Maggie had painstakingly put together, I was impressed by how many she'd done. She had been writing several years before considering having any serious demos produced, which is good because the more you write, the better you get, and the more chance you have of unearthing some real gems.

Although she can hold a tune well, Maggie added the vocal melodies on her workstation instead of singing them, using a lead instrument to hold the vocal line. This novel approach meant I had to read the lyrics along with the music, but it worked well. I don't think I've met anyone who approaches the songwriting and recording process identically. There is no right or wrong method, just the one that works best for you.

After listening to the songs, we narrowed it down to one called *Seventeen*. I agreed to play and record all the instruments, and so transform her backing track into a living, breathing song.

Maggie's approach was to write with an artist in mind. And when it came to *Seventeen* she asked, "Can you sound anything like James Blunt?" Fortunately, of all the people my singing voice has been compared to, it's him. Some days just feel like a divine set-up.

Suitably confident that I could make this happen, I set about playing, singing, and mixing what was Maggie's first song and, professionally speaking, mine, too. In the eleven years since that moment, together we've produced over fifty more, spanning blues, rock, pop, jazz, and folk.

These would never have happened had Maggie not demonstrated what it is to have true creative courage. It would have been easier for her to have stayed home that evening back in February 2010. But she chose courage, and because of that now has five full studio albums under her belt, a charity single, had songs played on the radio, been interviewed multiple times, been featured in a couple of books, and in a magazine (with one of her songs included on the cover CD).

She is still writing and producing songs well over a decade later. You can visit her website to hear them: songsforsingers.co.uk

This story proves you are capable of amazing things if you don't let fear be the adjudicator on what you can and cannot create. What you believe to be your limitations need not limit you. And it's never too late to share your work with others.

For twenty-eight years Maggie and Hugh ran retail shops in some of the UK's most historic towns and cities, including Edinburgh, Lincoln, and York. Their York shop, the one I knew, was on The Shambles, the city's most ancient street, and one of the few streets that gets a mention in the medieval Domesday Book.[1]

Maggie told me, "I was in retail management for far too many years, working all hours. I was becoming more stressed by the day, and songwriting became my way of escaping into another world. Now, if I'm in the midst of writing a song, I can't wait to get up and get on with it."

As well as transforming her own life, Maggie's artistic bravery continues to create opportunities for other creative people, too, as we often enlist session musicians, especially singers. Vocalists we've had the joy of working with include graduates of The Liverpool Institute for Performing Arts co-founded by Paul McCartney, and The Royal Academy of Music in London. And three other of our session singers were at one time or another signed to record labels in their own right.

I've met and worked with scores of high-calibre, hard-working, creative people, many of whom I now count as friends. Some, including Maggie and Hugh, were guests when Sarah and I were married. This demonstrates how creative desire mixed with relentless bravery dramatically changes the course of our lives.

I look back on those years in the barn with affection, although it was tough going. To help keep costs down, I didn't even have an internet connection. Instead, once every few days, I would take my laptop to a local coffee shop to process email and transfer files. This also doubled as my social life. I know it sounds sad, but the simplicity and restriction helped me focus, freeing up more time to work and hone my craft.

The barn was beautifully cool during hot summer days thanks to its porous insulation, although this meant the winters were freezing. I've never been so cold. Some days I'd work in the studio wearing thermal everythings, two pairs of jeans, multiple thick hoodies, two hats, and a sleeping bag draped over my knees. And that was with the heating on.

Speaking of heating, not many other recording studios

could boast an open fire, but I had one. It stood at the far end of the big room, and on winter evenings, I would burn anything I could get hold of. I'd then sit and stare silently into the flames, and contemplate the surreality that had become my life.

How would it all turn out?

It was hard, but it was an adventure, and I could feel myself coming alive.

After trying the best methods I knew to make life work, I had found myself with no work colleagues, a disintegrated community group, my marriage was no more, the bank was empty, and I'd had to sell my home. This was never the plan.

And when it dawns on you that you are the common denominator in a series of undesirable events, you owe it to yourself to evaluate how much of the chaos was down to you. It takes mettle to explore these questions and face your answers honestly because the implications might change your life in ways you weren't looking for – which is why many people avoid going there. But this reluctance to face themselves is why some artists never find boldness in their work.

Avoiding fear is never the path to bravery.

The collision of worlds with Maggie, and our ongoing working relationship, did not come about because we both exuded fearless confidence, or because our lives were perfect. It had everything to do with raw courage, from both parties. This is what happens when creative bravery in one person meets it in another, although I didn't feel particularly courageous at the time. I simply pointed myself in the direction I wanted to go and took a step, and then another. Courage is the decision to grow and move forward, no matter what.

However challenging things become, if we maintain our imagination, we always have a chance. Creative thinkers like you and I dream up options. We see different directions and hatch ingenious ideas. We combine familiar things in novel ways and we sculpt the future.

Be as inventive as you can with the resources you have. Keep that potent imagination of yours receptive and you'll flood your soul with belief.

Oftentimes nobody sees the fight. Nobody saw Maggie sick with anxiety. Nobody saw me freezing. When there are no friends, family, or colleagues to acknowledge your inner wars or see your victory over them, you must be your own witness. And that's okay, glorious even. Because when you don't need anyone else to validate your victory, no one has the power to take it from you.

So, in all your choosing, choose courage.

In all your creating, create courageously.

There's little to match the feeling of finding renewed strength when everything seems lost.

Brave And Beautiful

There was a time when nothing was beautiful.

Right up until 1526, in fact.

This was the year that the scholar William Tyndale smuggled his illegal translation of The New Testament into England. The printed words of these pages are where the word *beautiful* makes its first appearance within the English language.

Fittingly for the man who invented the word *beautiful*, Tyndale's writing itself possesses a pleasingly elegant quality, and many of his words and phrases have endured to become woven into the fabric of everyday speech, in much the same way as those of the famed playwright William Shakespeare.

Born in 1564, twenty-eight years after Tyndale's death, Shakespeare is credited with introducing over 1,700 words to the English-speaking world. Familiar phrases that originated with the man known as the Bard Of Avon include: *all that glitters is not gold*, *parting is such sweet sorrow*, and, of course, *to be, or not to be, that is the question.*

We are quick to celebrate Shakespeare and his contribution, and rightly so. However, although Tyndale – a student of both Oxford and Cambridge Universities – is not acknowledged in anything like the same way as Shakespeare, he too is responsible for inventing many words and phrases we still use every day; and some would argue he is the most influential of the two.

Can you imagine a world without *beautiful*?

Or phrases like *fight the good fight*, *a law unto themselves*, *signs of the times*, *the salt of the earth*, *filthy lucre*, *seek and ye shall find*, and *the powers that be.*

These are all Tyndale.

It is obvious that he took care when crafting these pithy, poetic phrases that now trip off the tongue with familiar ease. Much of his writing is monosyllabic, made up of simple words tastefully combined. They follow the cadence of everyday speech, but with a more considered use of rhythm and word choice, in a way that elevates the ordinary and points the reader toward the transcendent.

And it seems to me he didn't simply want to make a collection of ancient writings more widely available and accessible, but also for the words and sentences themselves to carry beauty and hope to the souls of everyday people.

Up until the point of Tyndale's translation work from Greek and Hebrew into English, The Bible had only been available in Latin, and only a few people were able and authorised to read it. As a result, most people were reliant on churchmen to interpret and present its contents. Tyndale fought both the church and government to create a translation in common language for the English people so they could read it for themselves and hear it read in their native tongue, a conviction that ultimately he gave his life to defend.

This was a fight to bring mass communication in an attractive way to all people and not just the rich, well-educated, or governmental leaders, many of whom didn't like the idea of giving up the power that exclusivity had afforded them. In light of this, it is interesting to notice that his new word *beautiful* appears in the gospel of Matthew where Jesus likened a sect of pious religious leaders to white-washed tombs – beautiful on the outside, but housing the stench of death inside.

Tyndale's translations, beginning with The New Testament, were printed in Germany before he smuggled them into his homeland. The authorities, under the kingship of Henry VIII, considered this a heretical act. And it was for this crime that, at age 42, Tyndale met his untimely demise. Following a betrayal and arrest, he was tried on the charge of heresy and found guilty.

On October 6, 1536, William Tyndale was throttled and his body burned at the stake. He was allowed a few last words, which were to cry out a prayer that God would open the King of England's eyes. And it so happened that within a matter of years, King Henry VIII authorised a version of the Bible based on Tyndale's translation. It was made available in parishes throughout his native England, and much of it became the foundation for the King James Bible that appeared almost a century later and is still hugely popular today.

For Tyndale, his work was more important than even the threat to his life. For the many of us who crumble at the hint of a bad review or critical comment, we will find that our creative life becomes more robust, more fulfilling, and less vulnerable to criticism once we engage with work so important to us it becomes the hill we are willing to die on. I hope this never happens in a literal sense, but you get the point. Higher rewards are often partnered with higher stakes.

What would it take for you, like Tyndale, to give your life to a creative work that demands your technical excellence, a love for and understanding of the people you serve, innovation within your discipline's vocabulary, resilience to keep going for years in order to see the work through, and bravery enough to defy the established authorities?

As creative people, our aim should be to lock into an underlying sense of purpose, and work from a place of love for others – not just ourselves – and mix that with a desire for learning, invention, and poetic beauty. Each of these things is a good thing in its own right, but pull them all together so that they work synergistically and you will hit a sweet spot, one that is far more than the sum of its parts and which may even put you on the path of your life's work.

It demands courage and conviction to take on such a large task as Tyndale did, and especially to complete it with admirable creative eloquence, all the while knowing that doing so was a crime punishable by death. His dream of bringing to common people the truth in which he so strongly believed was eventually realised, even though regrettably it was after he'd left the earth. What a tragic waste of a gifted and creative mind. Can you imagine eavesdropping on the conversation that might have happened between him and Shakespeare?

So, the next time you catch yourself discussing the powers that be, or describe someone as the salt of the earth, remember how the creative innovation of just one individual with deep-seated courage has the power to transform the world. Remember William Tyndale.

His bravery gave us *beautiful*.

What will yours bring?

The Nature Of Beauty

The pull toward beauty is the pull of the heart. It reminds us that we are human.

In *Till We Have Faces,* C. S. Lewis wrote, "The sweetest thing in all my life has been the longing – to reach the Mountain, to find the place where all the beauty came from – "

If you never notice beauty, you will never find the place where it all came from. In fact, if you never notice beauty, you will never even experience the longing to find its source; and what might have become the sweetest thing in all your life will pass you by entirely.

Beauty is there to be noticed.

Much like its bane, ugliness.

And presenting ugliness in a glamorous way makes it no less ugly. Somehow it makes it even more sinister.

Have you noticed how most news programmes now start with a dramatic blockbuster-film-style theme tune, introduced by a perfectly toothed host who spins us tale after tale about the current state of hell on earth. It is shiny, polished, and immaculately presented, with production values that would make an action movie jealous. There is a grotesque fascination about it that makes it hard to look away. But look away we must, and retrain our focus on higher things.

There was once a time that news reporting was a moral obligation in the service of humanity. Today, it's more of a relentless sensationalist entertainment show. The lines are often blurry, making it unclear what is news and what is intended for pleasure or amusement. It seems designed to entertain and scare us in equal measure. Like a horror movie.

It isn't limited to TV, either. The June 4, 2021 edition of USA Today was wrapped in a fake cover that, to all intents, looked real other than the small text toward the top of the page that reads: "ADVERTISEMENT".

This fake cover ran the shocking story of hybrid part-human, part-animal babies that posed "a threat to national security", which on closer inspection turned out to be an attention-grabbing advertising campaign by Netflix for its new show *Sweet Tooth*.[1]

To the undiscerning or unwary, it is becoming increasingly hard to determine the difference between fact and fiction. This leads to confusion, and distracts us from noticing all that is good and pleasing – much of which is readily available to us right here, right now.

Whenever something has your attention, question if you are being caught up in it, or are being captured by it. This will help you discern whether it is something worth engaging with, or in the case of your work, something worth creating and sharing.

There is a difference between captivating and captivity.

Beauty captivates. Whereas entertainment and faux news tend to hold us captive.

The never-ending stream of bad news and shock-factor art and music is making things look uglier than they are and giving the impression that everything is out of control. It is changing minds to believe in the inevitability of things worsening. I don't believe this is true, but proportionately few others seem to agree. This is why we need an artistic rebellion – not to propagate another message as such, but simply to be beautiful.

Art is transformational when it brings beauty into ugly places.

If you know of an ugly place, whether it be physical, mental, or spiritual, then you know a place that is thirsting for a revelation of beauty. Whenever you battle the notion that there cannot surely be room for you or your creative work – whatever guise it may take – the existence of ugliness is proof enough that we need you, your art, and your creative mind.

Even if you are crushed with self-doubt or limited in some other way, this remains true. If the restrictions of time, relationships, or physical incapacity constrain you, and you are unable to make anything – let alone anything you consider beautiful – it is still possible to leave your mark and make a worthwhile difference.

How?

Simply draw another human being's attention to something beautiful.

It is easy to do.

All you need are the three simple words we learned as kids when crossing the road: *stop, look, listen*.

This is a powerful creative act in itself. Do this and you will help others lift their eyes, stir their curiosity, encourage them to ask questions, and discover hope – sometimes for the first time. If you know someone who has lost sight of the beautiful, the best thing you can do is point them back toward it.

Sir Roger Scruton is right when he says, "Beauty is vanishing from our world because we live as though it did not matter."[2]

When something doesn't matter to us, we pay little attention to it. And our negligence is leaving us bereft. It is not healthy for society to neglect something that is so good for the soul.

It's as though there is a conspiracy against beauty in the elevated name of functionality. Swathes of grey, square, utilitarian buildings house the places we live, work, recreate, and worship. Whether uniform apartments, big box stores, or shopping website warehouses, none of these seem to be built for a purpose beyond utility and flexibility. There is no soul or character baked into them based on their unique mission. They are just veneer-topped modular infrastructures made to adapt easily to whoever next takes residence.

Some modern buildings are so grid-like and contourless you can't even find the door without effort. You never have that kind of trouble with an old manor house or cathedral. Their grand arched entrances leave you in no doubt as to how to get in, and lend you a certain dignity merely by crossing their threshold.

Beauty is both useful and ennobling.

My family and I live in sight of the Snowdonia mountains. In winter, when snow falls, you'd think we lived on the outskirts of Narnia. I often wonder why these mountains are here. It's like asking what a sunset is for. Or a starry sky. They serve no real pragmatic purpose, yet they nourish the soul far more than a functional apartment block ever could.

True beauty is harmonious and complementary without

being boring or predictable. Uniform and utilitarian design is always unpleasantly sterile, and has a knack of sucking the life from your soul. You know you're in a place built on the cheap, or with the worst scenarios in mind, when it is obvious nobody chose the decor and furnishings based on making people feel good. Instead, they prioritised things being low cost, easy to clean, and hard wearing.

And take house designs, for example. Although new houses are built with all the modern gadgets, many are paper thin. You may be able to control the heating and peek out of your front doorbell's security camera from your phone, but you can't sing in the shower without waking up your next-door neighbour.

If you live in an aesthetically depressing place, why not do something to change it. Perhaps you could start a gallery. You might not even need a building. For example, I remember when the already beautiful English city of York beautified its streets further by hanging weatherproof reproductions of famous paintings on the outdoor walls of shops, pubs, and churches, effectively turning the city into an open-air gallery.

Displays of beauty are signs of life. Without our caring and creative touch, the quirks and whims we enjoy and identify with as part of being human will eventually meld into stupefying and restrictive uniformity. This is why we need to contribute as much beauty as we can to the world.

Even if you feel you can't contribute anything beautiful to where you are, will you at least resist being part of its uglification?

Simply avoid ugly things and promote those that are not.

While I appreciate the need for commentary on life and acknowledgement of the dark side of things, I'm not an advocate of using creativity and the arts to shock purely for the sake of it. For this to be your approach, it seems you must constantly become weirder or more deviant than whatever came beforehand, and it appears many artists and creators are engaged in this ethos of needing to become ever more strange.

The alarm bells ring for me here because this bizarre race to the bottom is the antithesis of maturation and development, and is more like the trajectory of the addict. When the 'gateway drug' of the initial experience no longer satisfies, things must get more intense, harder, riskier, and weirder if the artist is to experience any feeling toward their work, because they've become so calloused and sensitively dull over time.

Whenever the attraction to something can be more accurately named as repulsion, we replace the appreciation of beauty with the allure of lust. And lust's propensity toward impulsivity is all about consuming something we are drawn to and getting a hit from it as quickly as possible.

I can always tell when my soul has become chronically deprived of beauty because I start craving biscuits. And chocolate. And chocolate biscuits. My coffee consumption goes up and I need to buy a new guitar, or ideally three. The voices of lust, addiction, and compulsion all want to be heard. And if I acquiesce and choose to feed the beast, I contribute to the continuation of the cycle. I intensify the darkness, all the while maintaining my separation from what I really need.

Beauty is different.

Beauty doesn't take, but gives. It doesn't tear down, but builds up. However, beauty does require long-term appreciation, a dwelling upon. And beauty must be fought for. And tended to.

And so the brave artist's call is to defy the cultural bias toward the quick, easy, and crude, and instead create works of unaffected beauty that satisfy, not just gratify.

It is one thing to present something that captures the attention temporarily, but quite another to create something for the soul that is good and lasting.

"What is needed is not an ugly protest but a beautiful song," writes author Brian Zahnd.[3]

Great art strengthens the heart. It fortifies the spirit and infuses it with hope. Beauty is a core facet of life that makes it worth living. If you remove beauty, you take away the essence of what it is to be human. This could be why some of the most expensive artefacts money can buy are works of great art.

Remove art from the people and you remove the heart of the people. The presence of beauty does something to bolster human resilience, and its absence is demoralising. Perhaps this is why Hitler had many pieces of artwork seized and hidden or destroyed. In total, Nazis are purported to have confiscated 16,000 'degenerate' works of art.[4]

Whenever you are tempted to think your art doesn't matter, remember that one aspect of a world takeover strategy included quashing the beautiful and quelling the inspirational. The war over beauty is a war over the thriving of the human soul, of its dignity, and its value.

Beauty is about experience and encounter. A meeting with another person is enhanced by the purposeful introduction of beauty. It is a gesture of moving toward the other with reverence, and dignifies the interaction with the desire to make it subjectively more pleasing.

When you attend a wedding, for example, you present yourself in a way that appropriately honours the couple and the occasion. If you have friends round for a meal, you might carefully lay out your best tablecloth, plates, and matching cutlery. When visiting a relative in hospital, you wear your best smile, and bring them a bunch of flowers, because the beauty of the flowers offers cheerfulness and hope.

Remove the flowers and hope dies a little. Remove the cheer that beauty brings, and you amplify desperation.

So, keep giving beauty as a gift because intentionally shared beauty holds meaning and is an expression of honour and dignity. It's not pragmatic or utilitarian. And that is the point. It is soul. It is spirit. It is an expression of love from one to another. Healthy people are all alike in their desire to adorn the world with beauty in some way, not least because of the strong natural bond that unifies beauty and honour.

So, I invite you to join me in opposing the proliferation of ugliness, as we instead flood the world with beauty wherever and whenever we can.

Proper Art Or Propaganda

I wrote these words in the year 5781. True story.

But how so?

You'd be forgiven for thinking I'd taken a secret sci-fi obsession a little too far and written this book while convinced I was a visitor from the future. Although an understandable conclusion, it would be wrong. The truth is, this book and I are from another epoch. A parallel dimension. Kind of.

Oh, okay. I'm actually using a different calendar.

Most of us organise our lives according to the Gregorian calendar, a solar dating system that has been with us since 1582, and is based on the earth's journey around the sun. But other methods are in use. The Hebrew calendar, for example (which is lunisolar, meaning that it tracks with the natural cycles of both the sun and the moon) is a fascinating system in which the years and decades are assigned a theme according to their number.

For instance, the year 2020, which we will all remember for its pandemic hysteria, emergency restrictions, and global lockdowns, coincided with the Hebrew year 5780, which marked the beginning of the decade of the mouth.

Intriguingly, as this decade of the mouth began, many things pertaining to the mouth – and by extension speech, communication, and declaration – were shut down all around the world: theatre stopped, live music stopped, congregational singing stopped, social gatherings stopped, and group conversations stopped; masks concealed smiles as they muffled voices, which were further quietened behind plastic guards, screens, and booths; social media posts and videos were checked for factual accuracy, and many were subsequently removed. Some people were banned entirely from their online accounts.

This striking series of events all happened at the same time. During the decade of the mouth.

The creative mind continually notices patterns and themes. It subconsciously connects the dots and wants to know what their relationship might mean until eventually either an epiphany or a question emerges.

I point these things out to invite us into new, inquisitive avenues of thought, and I leave the interpretation open.

What do you think about it? Is it all mere chance? Co-incidence? Or are unseen forces manoeuvring things beneath the surface?

I ask because, now more than ever, I am convinced we need to wonder and explore with eyes wide open, and yet I sense a resistance growing against untethered, imaginative creativity.

It's not that aesthetics aren't at play in the world. They clearly are. We cannot move without a polished media assault on our senses from somewhere. But to what end? We are inundated with information and preoccupied with low-grade amusement, the deluge serving to dumb us down and numb us out. And so we respond to our stupor by exposing ourselves to yet more stimulation, hoping it will do something to wake us up. But it doesn't. And drip by drip we oversaturate until eventually our souls can take in no more.

And here we are, grossly overstimulated and profoundly unmoved.

The repetition leaves us dull and inert, chiefly because the creative work we're exposed to isn't really art. It's more of an art-like substance. Much like the foods that hold nothing of nutrition are, to be more accurate, more of a food-like substance. They are attractively packaged and alluring, boasting sound-bite slogans that lodge in your brain; and they are also addicting and bad for your health.

Consider this: all things being equal, when choosing tonight's evening meal, would you prefer something mass-produced and microwaved or home-grown and homemade?

I would argue the same question is valid regarding the art, entertainment, and media we ingest.

Because wherever true art is made, there lurks a convincing imitation looking to usurp it. Just as the carrot and stick subjugate the donkey, creative aesthetics beguile the unwary. Images, words, and music enhance an already seductive narrative, as together they subliminally condition us to be scared of the stick while hoping one day we'll reach that carrot. This is the artful use of threat and reward, fear and desire, manufactured manipulation designed to influence your thoughts, not delight your soul. It is more propaganda than proper art.

When selling a house, was it by chance the seller happened to be baking bread and brewing fresh coffee as the viewings began? Of course not. They were doing all they could to sell their property, manipulating the senses to encourage others to do what they wanted them to do. Obviously, they wouldn't want to show the place in a terrible light, but there's a fine line between presenting something at its best and manipulating aesthetics to twist someone's arm.

How can you tell the difference? Just ask yourself if someone is opening a door for you, or if they are trying to shove you through it.

Certain types of advertising and marketing brazenly attempt the latter. You will recognise it whenever the choice you are given feels like no choice at all. How often do you hear orchestral strings attempt to pull your heartstrings in the hope you'll open your purse strings? It is easy to get cynical and jaded, but, when wrapped up in seductive packaging, the continued efforts to cajole can be hard to discern and resist.

But resist you must, because the world needs your art – your real art. And we need your voice – your real one.

"Art opposes tyranny by freeing beauty from the clutches of the powers of this world," says J. F. Martel in *Reclaiming Art in the Age of Artifice.*

And this highlights our role as creatives and artists: we are conduits, reconnecting heavy hearts back to hope. We rejoin the disassociated with reality. The beauty we share reveals truth beyond fact.

The ugliness of societal and political feuding is tiring. People long to find genuine places of reverence, hope, and wonder.

When beauty is hijacked and used to surreptitiously hide ideologies, agendas, and moral codes, it acts like poison laced within sugar. Bait and switch. When the promise of sweetness delivers a wormwood aftertaste, we learn to distrust beauty altogether because we've seen it lie. And now beauty is ruined.

It's not that art with an agenda is intrinsically bad. I'm not even sure art without an agenda exists. There's always some kind of reason behind it. Even the advocate of *art for art's sake*, by promoting the idea, is inescapably supporting an agenda. So perhaps we should pay more attention to understanding the nature of the motive behind the art, not the fact a motive exists. Because not all are nefarious, even if we don't happen to share the same views as the artist. It's easy to interpret the art of those we don't agree with as being propaganda just because they've created from a specific perspective, and that perspective is different from ours.

Even so, we must be sharp-eyed and keen of ear, discerning and alert. The creative voice originates in the mind, and not every thought we have is our own. Other voices seek to infiltrate our thought stream, demanding attention, seeking our allegiance, and are quick to scoff and eager to mock if we neglect their party line or fall out of step.

But out of step is exactly where you will find the artist.

In order to speak, to say a new thing, a true thing, to offer original work, and disrupt the cult of culture, the artist must by necessity break with convention. Because conventional is not original. And no matter your medium, your creative voice must aim to be original, because this is what sets you apart as worthy of remark and attention. The unique expression of your perspective is the platform from which you speak, paint, compose, write. Otherwise, you're a cover band. A look-alike. A cheap knock-off.

And yet the culture encourages us to use only approved terminology, and not say what we really want to say. If our semantics are deemed wrong, the spirit of what we meant goes ignored. Euphemisms replace truth. But you cannot be the next Dickens if you write from a phrase book. And our voices are weakened if our language is curtailed.

Along these lines, Madeleine L'Engle soberly warns us of the vulnerabilities this can lead to, "If our vocabulary dwindles to a few shopworn words, we are setting ourselves up for takeover by a dictator."[1]

In *What Is Art?* Leo Tolstoy writes a remarkable author's preface, dated 29 March 1898, in which he expresses his frustration about earlier versions of this work being censored. "A book has appeared under my name containing thoughts attributed to me which are not mine."[2]

It is extraordinary to think a man we regard as one of our greatest ever writers should have his thoughts on art so edited that he no longer recognised them as his own. Tolstoy was disheartened at being unable to share his observations and original thoughts without having them regulated.

Hearing that, our minds may quickly go to the political

arena, or the religious, as we point our bony fingers and apportion blame as to why we think we are creatively frustrated. But sometimes the biggest oppressor of our creative lives isn't sitting in the halls of office.

Sometimes, we ourselves are the tyrant.

A good start would be owning up to the bullying we subject ourselves to, and finally take responsibility for our own work. And it is this need to take personal responsibility that makes freedom so challenging.

Most of us would be quick to say we'd like more freedom to create. But freedom costs. Are we willing to make sacrifices to gain and maintain that freedom? Not everyone is.

Many are happy with bread and circuses as their lot. So long as there is always something on the table and the TV there's no cause to think overly hard, or invent, or dream. *Keep 'em fed and entertained and they're no trouble.* Plus, following the experts makes things simpler. Okay, it may not be freedom exactly, but it is easy. And we like easy.

Don't we?

This is all well and good if you're happy with how things are and where they are going. But I'm of the mind that repeating our past is no way of preparing ourselves and our children for the world that is coming.

Start small if you need to, but do start. If you have no

platform to the world, begin with your country, or your town, or your street, your family, your friends. Return to folk tales and songs from real people, not just the narrative fed us by the establishment. Because the mainstream isn't always the right stream.

Convince don't coerce. Be honest, and ever humble, discerning not judging. Know well the place you create from, and be candid about your reasons.

Your creative work will satiate hunger in people they didn't even know they had. It has the power to turn conflict into conversation, bringing joy, delight, and freedom to hearts who have only a vague memory left of what that all means. Your art can provide alternate interpretations, insights, perspectives, and ideologies that could better suit and serve people, if only they were given the chance to hear them.

And for some, yours is the voice they've been waiting for. Yours is the art that speaks. They have ears to hear if only you'd say something.

What will you do with this opportunity you've been given?

What will you do with your voice?

What say you?

Break The (Jelly) Mould

The celebrated post-impressionist painter Vincent Van Gogh once said, "If you hear a voice within you say 'you cannot paint,' then by all means paint and that voice will be silenced."[1]

In other words, by presenting itself as opposition, the voice that claims you cannot create, inadvertently insists that you must. Respond to it well and you become stronger, while it unwittingly sows the seeds of its own destruction. Its naysaying urges you to become more resourceful, waking you up to where you are and what you've got. It stimulates creative thinking, which, in turn, generates options. Options give you choice, and choice brings freedom. And the foremost expression of that freedom is unencumbered creativity.

Therefore, in times of restriction and opposition, don't abandon your imagination. Whatever you do, don't do that. You need it all the more. Its lens gives you sight beyond the immediate and helps you prepare for what is coming. You can see it in your mind's eye. This kind of imagining is the purveyor of hope because of the new possibilities it generates. You start to dream again and envisage previously unseen ways of seeing and doing things.

Along these lines, those who live the creative life are kith and kin to the sage. They reach deep into unseen realms to pull back beautiful and essential treasures of wisdom on behalf of the rest of us. Whether musician or mystic, poet or prophet, each uses the same interior mechanisms with which to see, dream, and proclaim their revelations, often in creative and conspicuous ways.

As the world distracts itself with tall tales and masquerades, more than ever, we need creative truth-tellers with the courage to be a mouth, not just a mouthpiece. Creation aches for artists who are willing to look deeply, with unveiled eyes, and then declare with audacity the things they've seen in their visions beyond the veil.

This is where the courage to be creative and conspicuous comes to the fore. Because to look and sound the same as the masses only reinforces the cultural trance.

So pay no more attention to the fakes, flakes, and attention seekers, those who clamour for the light in lust of adulation. But heed the ones who stand in darkness and burn their lives down like a candle so that others might find their way.

This work of bringing light into the shadows is a grave responsibility because your art carries influence. Never create intending to coerce. Never manipulate others into giving up their sovereignty or power, leaving them less than they were beforehand. No matter how aesthetically beautiful it may be, propaganda in the guise of art, wilfully deployed to shape reality, is a wretched thing.

Media specifically made for screens are some of the most culpable, and effective, because the experience takes place subliminally. Watch any film, marketing, news, or entertainment and notice how much more like being in a dream it is than when observing real life.

By contrast, books, for example, are more participatory and interactive. When we read, we actively imagine, and in some sense, we work to co-create with the author.

We engage far less actively with the cinematic but are instead passively receptive and thus more suggestible. In front of a screen, we connect more on the level of the subconscious than the intellectual, engaging the mechanisms of instinctual belief over logical rationale. This isn't a bad thing in itself, but we must be aware it is happening and that we are susceptible.

Are we being entertained or trained?

When we've grown to trust a particular source, we believe what we are told, and especially what we are shown. As we experience feelings of empathy, sympathy, rage, or fear concerning certain scenarios or philosophies over and again, our emotions open us up to a message that may eventually change our minds without our realising.

At home, we have a jelly mould in the shape of a teddy bear. Whatever we pour into it and allow to set comes out shaped like that bear. Be it jelly, mud, sand – whatever. No matter what we pour into it, everything comes out the same shape. You make a mould by first pushing a solid object into a softer, malleable material: steel pushed into clay, for example. This makes a detailed hollow impression, which is where you pour the liquid that you want to shape and solidify.

Similarly, we acquire our mindsets from pouring our thoughts into the mould formed by the impressions that have been made upon us. When our emotions soften, our thoughts liquify and can be formed or reformed, taking the shape of the mould we submit them to, and then when hardened, they emerge in an entirely different shape.

Our minds are formed through information, a word that has its roots in the Latin *informare* meaning to give form or shape to.

The information we receive has as much to do with shaping our thinking as it does communicating facts or relaying instructions. It moulds our perspective, our worldview, and our thoughts, influencing the core places we create from.

If the things we let inform us are ultimately what form

us, the question, therefore, is, what do we want to shape our thinking? How do we want our minds to be formed?

Whatever makes an impression *on* us shapes the expression *from* us.

And as a culture, we are being shaped into accepting a video game life.

The deluge of phones, tablets, laptops, earbuds, virtual reality headsets, and so on, are leading us to experience more of life entirely within our brains, and less of it embodied as contributing participants in the real world. Wherever you go, take the time to watch the people you happen upon. They're transfixed; senses engulfed by an overload of images, icons, flashes, and affirming beeps and buzzes.

People are becoming automatons, drowning in a button-pressing, screen-swiping hypnosis. This mesmerising delusion we see lulling the masses to sleep is a counterfeit, and we'd be wise to sidestep it. Otherwise, we risk being locked into a world where addiction usurps astonishment and freedom of thought gives way to groupthink.

And no great works of art were ever made as a result of groupthink. Nor were fulfilling lives. So if you desire to create from an authentic place, you cannot afford to be passive in this area.

Don't concede the shaping of your mind to the chaos of the culture.

Soul Trader

How much would you pay to be considered great?

Let's travel back to 1930s America to hear about a bluesman and his alleged pact with the devil.

As a young man, Robert Leroy Johnson, born in rural Mississippi around 1911, longed to be a Delta blues guitarist and singer. The problem being he wasn't particularly gifted. So, according to the legend, he had a midnight meeting at a Mississippi crossroads with the devil himself, who gave Johnson an unearthly mastery of the guitar in exchange for his soul.

Johnson then disappeared from town for around a year, and on his return could do things with a guitar no one else could match.

Despite only ever recording 29 songs, Robert Johnson became a giant of the blues, and influenced many significant musicians of later generations. Pioneers in their own right such as Bob Dylan, The Rolling Stones, and Led Zeppelin include themselves on the long list of his admirers. Eric Clapton went as far as to say Johnson was "the most important blues singer that ever lived."[1]

So how was a man able to transform from amateur to master so quickly? Perhaps he'd spent his reclusive year practising day and night. Or was something supernatural at play? As documentation of Johnson's life is patchy and veiled in mystery, no one seems to know for sure what happened. But a dramatic transformation undeniably took place.

Although, unfortunately, it didn't last long.

While Johnson did get his wish of becoming a brilliant and influential musician, the deal he'd made was high stakes, and it wasn't long before the debt was called in.

Robert Leroy Johnson died in 1938, aged 27, amidst rumours he'd been poisoned. This gives him the dubious honour of being one of the first members – if not the founding member – of *The 27 Club*, a curious collective of musicians and singers who all died at the same tragically young age.

Whether you encounter the devil himself, or incarnate in some big-shot executive who marks you as a malleable and marketable commodity, ask yourself this: if you get your talent and platform from another, will they want it back? And what do they want from you in return? History is strewn with tales of creators and artistic visionaries exploited by unscrupulous taskmasters. Promised the world, they were given hell after being convinced by the fairytale that: "This is for your own good. We'll keep you safe and manage things better than you can, just hand over control. You can trust us – we're experts."

A believable lie can turn a gift into a curse.

Don't take your alliances and allegiances lightly. Weigh them with sobriety. Have the courage to walk away from anything you suspect is a fool's bargain, because the pay-off is never worth what you surrender.

Crossroads demand a choice. This is where roads meet, paths intersect, and destinies are decided.

Whether you believe the tale of Robert Johnson's diabolical deal to be true or folklore, it still raises questions brave artists must answer.

What is success?

What are you willing to sacrifice to get it, and who to?

How much sacrifice is too much?

Surely it cannot be worth gaining the whole world only to lose your soul.

Actively Still

Brave artists stand against the tide.

Any dead fish can go with the flow.

As the prevailing current sweeps it downriver, the dead fish remains thoroughly passive, and only goes where it is taken. Yet the big rock that lies fixed to the bed of that same river defies all pressure to move. It is still. If we can achieve a similar rock-like inner stability, our circumstances become the minor factor. We get first claim on who we are and how we feel, not anybody or anything else. The aim is to achieve stillness, which may seem to imply inactivity but is, in reality, an active resistance.

Every day, emotionally charged information is thrown at us, subliminally looking to shape us. The round-the-clock bombardment of fear-inducing news can easily overwhelm, promoting concern about the future and our place in it. It is tempting to want to numb out, with entertainment the first place we go. But trying to achieve stillness by letting entertainment wash over us doesn't work. We become no less still and train ourselves to become mentally passive.

And passivity is not stillness.

In 2003 I did serious damage to my ankle while playing football, and for a couple of months I had regular sessions with a sports physio. Part of my rehab programme was to balance on one leg while a moving platform rotated beneath my foot. To stay still and not fall off, I continually had to reposition my ankle to be in the right spot.

This is being actively still.

To the onlooker I was stationary, but maintaining this position was anything but a passive pursuance. It took a lot of effort to stay in the same place. I had to adjust my posture continually, otherwise I would hit the deck. To stay in place, I had to keep moving.

This is a helpful analogy for how to keep the mind still, clear, and calm, ready to create despite the swirling eddies of life. When everything surrounding you is in flux, you can't keep still by doing nothing. Your stability requires your movement. In our creative lives, we can build strength and remain upright by engaging in active stillness – adjusting and counterbalancing the forces that push against us.

Make it your business to become acutely aware of whatever is resisting you, nudging you, trying to topple you, then adjust and rebalance. Commit to making perpetual micro-adjustments. Focus. Even if your attention span would embarrass a goldfish, train yourself to focus; mentally tune out the static, and silence the turbulence. You are the final arbiter over what has meaning to you. Own your perspective and choose courageously.

Finding this place of internal equilibrium is key to accessing your most creative self. And the converse is also true: in times of acute anxiety or turmoil, having a creative practice is a powerful ally.

When under stress, we go into threat defence mode, which is when the small, almond-shaped part of our brain called the *amygdala* signals to our glands to pump stress hormones around our body, putting us into fight-flight-or-freeze mode. This is vital for our immediate survival, if, say, we're being chased by a disgruntled grizzly, but is much less helpful when switched on permanently.

If you are serious about your creative work but keep hitting a wall of anxiety, going deep with an alternate activity can be effective. Take up a fun, creative pursuit unrelated to your genre. Painting, drawing, collage, or playing an instrument work well. As you immerse yourself in something enjoyable and free of pressure, you'll naturally abandon the future-tripping that's behind your racing mind, giving your body time to calm and regulate. Do this as a regular practice to get into a good place before transitioning over to your real work.

Sometimes we must fool ourselves into reaching the state we want to be in. Willpower alone doesn't usually cut it. For instance, you can't will your heart to beat faster or slower, or make your pupils dilate; you can't start and stop your digestion at will; you can't fall asleep or wake up on demand. The body doesn't react to your conscious, logical mind in that way. But through a new creative practice you can sneak up on it, via your subconscious.

So, if you're feeling uncreative or wound up, try dancing before you paint, or drawing before you write. Allow yourself time and space to freely play and create. Before a race, a professional athlete will stretch and move and get into their zone beforehand. Think of your new creative practice in the same way, but less as a warm-up and more of an open-up.

Remember to be patient and kind with yourself, because the calming process isn't instant; but eventually, you will feel a lot better, be less reactive, and have a clear mind. This place of assured stability is where your true creative voice will emerge. So cultivating interior stillness is essential, especially if everything on the outside is mayhem. You don't need to empty your mind and make it as blank as possible, just simply focus on slowing it down. As you relax, you'll eventually tune into the voice of your heart. You'll imagine, and you'll remember.

When you don't even have time to finish a thought, let alone a piece of work, you know you need stillness. Just as the cabin crew on a flight reminds you that, in the case of an emergency, you must put on your own oxygen mask before trying to help another person, your relationship with yourself and your soul is vital to everything else. Never letting your mind slow down to drift is like forcing your body to run continually and then trying to speak while fighting for breath. When you've constantly pushed your soul, and are living in survival mode, deep communication goes out of the window, whether that is with yourself, with others, or with your art.

If you forgo slowing down, you never get to just sit and listen. And without listening, you won't know what to make, and, as a result, you'll lose the confidence to create.

So sit quiet a while, close your eyes, open your heart.

And listen.

You're about to discover things that you didn't know you knew.

You must discover what's in there – even though knowing can feel scary; even though you'd rather keep the mental noise turned up and the day's activities constant; even though, granted, if you keep on pushing you will achieve a lot of busy work and get a lot of things done.

But how will you know they were the *right* things if you never took the time to listen?

There's Knowing And There's Knowing

You are brave when you admit you don't know.

And when you admit you don't know, you are open. Which is good. Because creativity needs your openness.

A curious mind delights in the wonder of each new discovery, and will excitedly lead others to witness the same revelation if they'll dare to come along. You will recognise these people by the way they direct their enthusiasm. They're the ones shouting "Look at this," rather than "Look at me."

Ideas, emotions, oxygen, love, atoms, hopes, thoughts, dark matter, spirit, quarks, memories, light: all these elements, and more, conspire and converge within the brushstroke of an artist, the word of a poet, or the bowed string of a violin. Any single creative act contains too much for one mind to fathom in one go.

Think on it long enough to think on it deeply, and you'll

be awestruck.

And "Awe is why we are here," said writer Anne Lamott.[1]

Which, I think, is the point. Or at least one of the good ones.

Learn to love the questions. You are allowed to have questions without having to resolve them.

Wherever we place false constraints on curiosity is where awe stops and the waning of our creativeness starts. This is when we stop asking further questions and lean on our experience instead; we presume to understand, and forget we can continually be astonished if we'd only pay attention. We forget to look and listen. We forget to ask. And then ask again.

It takes bravery to ask again because people might think we're ignorant. But so what? The more we ask, the more we learn, and the more we learn, the more nuance we notice, and the more nuance we notice, the more fantastical the mundane becomes.

This ability to see the nuanced hidden in plain sight is core to our creative calling. We use it to introduce people to what they never knew was always there, and we do this by paying attention to what everyone else has missed.

According to Einstein, anyone "… who can no longer pause to wonder and stand rapt in awe, is as good as dead; his eyes are closed."[2]

I'm a layman entirely, but I'm intrigued by just how interconnected everything and everybody is. Quantum physics explores this notion. As does spirituality. Science and faith are two worldviews often presented as being oppositional and mutually exclusive, but, done properly, they overlap and inform each other tremendously. Simplistically put, science explains some of the mechanics of what is going on, and faith helps us make sense of why. The intersection of the two is probably where our most complete understanding lies.

And, for me, this intersection is where true art resides.

Art reconciles the visible with the invisible. It grabs a hand from each realm, draws them ever closer until they touch, and keeps going until they clasp. This is where heaven meets quantum theory, and they kiss. This thin place makes known the unseen materials from which everything was first imagined and continues to be sustained. It is beautiful, miraculous, and ever so strange. Here, a curious communion develops as the mystic and the scientist marvel at all they've seen and just how much they've yet to learn.

This is the place I go to reconcile the unexplained and miraculous happenings in life.

A renewed sense of awe is also the starting place toward restoration from burn-out, and the cure for boredom, too. When you find yourself exhausted by the platitudes of other people's certainties, and you feel your strength grow faint as your creative flame flickers and fades, you can reignite your light by fiercely pursuing wide-eyed wonder.

And don't just focus on your particular craft. Go wider. See more, experience more.

And read more: what an affordable, accessible way books are to expand your mind. And if you happen to read a book that shuts you down then close it up. Not everything helps. I've read mystics so mystical that I can't work out how to ground their message or make use of it. I've read scientists so pragmatic that my joy of creative discovery would be all but destroyed if their analytical dissections were the only valid viewpoint. Even so, it is possible to learn something from everyone. If you'll allow them, everybody can teach you something. Take the elements that help you and don't worry about the rest.

I'm not suggesting you invest hours trawling through insufferable drivel, of course, although if you have the temperament, time, and tenacity then go for it. There are almost always gems worth digging for. Sometimes a single sentence will make an entire book worth the reading.

Here's the thing, which should be obvious but doesn't seem to be: creative people approach creative work creatively. You don't have to fit the 'correct' mould or adopt the 'right' way to be creative. There isn't one. We all sit at different points along a kind of creativity continuum. And we get to change seats at different times. The beauty is that whenever we move, we see things from a new angle, which leads to new insights as our viewpoint is adjusted.

Creative minds being what they are, keep discovering new things and new ways to do old things. The vista ever broadens.

Even more fun (or frustrating, depending on your view) is that many methods even seem contradictory. Do they all result in satisfyingly creative work? Yes. Does this mean there may be more than one effective approach? Oftentimes, yes. Don't you think it would be oxymoronic if there were only one?

We relate to our work according to who we are and when we are, both of which are constantly in flux. You're like a sailor at sea in a small vessel, so keep your eyes on the horizon of the truth as you undulate with every wild new wave of discovery you make.

Aim to be bold and confident without being obstinate and inflexible. The key to being creative is to remain teachable, not dogmatic. Prescriptive instructions are useful for repeating a discovery that has already been made: you get predictable results that way; and a step-by-step recipe is exactly what you need if, for example, you're running a restaurant with a consistent menu.

But there are no recipe books for those combinations yet

to be discovered. You have to invent those yourself. This is the essence of brave art. And this is why you're here.

If you've been holding back waiting for permission, here it is: I hereby give you permission to be courageously creative. So, now that lack of permission is no longer a valid excuse for you, go try something new. Make unusual combinations. If it's fixed, break it – see what happens.

The trick is to stay wide awake, paying attention, and rapt in awe. Can you do that?

Awesome.

Seeing Red, I Think

I needed a decent guitar. Especially if I was going to be a rock star.

Back in the late 1980s, many of the guitar players I aspired to emulate, such as Joe Satriani, Steve Vai, Reb Beach, and Paul Gilbert, all played Ibanez guitars. Whereas mine … mine was, well, it was cheap. It didn't inspire me and sounded average at best.

I had to have a professional-grade instrument. But for that I needed money. Quite a lot of it.

So my under-weight, over-haired bandmates and I had an idea: to spend a few weeks earning big bucks going tomato picking. We were determined to rack up weeks of hard graft to fund our dream instruments and land a record deal.

Colin had a car, so he was transport.

At 6 a.m. on our first morning at the tomato farm, or whatever it is they're called, four of us bleary-eyed teenagers were taken through our induction.

Thankfully, it wasn't too hard to grasp. When you break them down, the rules of tomato picking are pretty simple:

1. Find a ripe tomato
2. Pick it

To be fair, none of us expected it to go belly-up at this point, but you live and learn, don't you?

It turned out that Colin – our only way of getting to and from the tomato farm – was colour blind. He genuinely couldn't tell which of the fruit were ripe and which were not; and when your job is tomato picking, this quickly becomes something of an issue.

Rather gamely, Colin agreed to sit alone in his car for the whole day, while the rest of us cut our hands to shreds picking fruit for hours on end. It wasn't much fun either, as the tomato juice made the cuts sting like crazy, and I was secretly happy when our head of transport announced his retirement on the way home, thus forcing me to find another way to fund a guitar.

This silly little anecdote taught me a valuable life lesson, however: by relying too much on another person to get me where I wanted to go, I put myself at the mercy of their ability to see things as they truly were. If for some reason they were unable to see accurately, they had the power to derail my creative plans.

So, when you're writing your book or scoring your symphony, remember that the journey you're on should never, ever, be entrusted entirely to the hands of a colour-blind tomato picker.

It is deceptively easy to presume our perceptions are the same as one another's, and that what we're seeing must be what others are seeing, therefore making it true. But often, albeit in good faith and to the best of our knowledge, we operate out of presumption.

Colin and I knew what tomato picking was, and both of us knew we could pick baskets of them. We 'knew' a lot of things. So we didn't wonder about them, because we thought we knew. But this was a day of surprises. A day of revelation. A new part of Colin's larger story was unveiled, something he and his friends did not previously know: he couldn't accurately see light reflected at 650 nanometres.

I saw red but Colin saw green, and both of us were right, and both of us were ignorant of a larger truth at play. What we saw was contradictory yet undeniably true.

This incident caused each band member to question his perspective. Which is the kind of thing good art does. This is what our work will do, and this is what we'll regularly stumble across if we continually live in wonder. We'll go for decades creating out of a paradigm that unexpectedly explodes, catapulting us into a whole new realm, in which our previous worldview reduces to become only a part, and an interpretative part at that.

American film producer Robert Evans is quoted as saying, "There are three sides to every story: your side, my side, and the truth. And no one is lying."[1]

There are facts. And there is truth.

Whenever you discover something that works, remember it may be just a fact and not a truth. Factual approaches work because of the truths they're built upon. They don't shape the truth but are interpretations of it. Facts are contingent on the perspective and framework they are presented within, and they may be subject to change.

There is always a wider narrative that underpins the anecdote. In other words, a truth exists that upholds the facts. As creative people, we must hold the truth firmly and our interpretation lightly.

When we create, and especially when we are in the zone, our focus of attention forms a kind of frame around our work. It becomes all that we see. We are blinkered. This deep, singular concentration gives us a chance of producing something worthwhile. However, the frame that restrains scattered thinking also limits our view of the bigger picture. The larger story disappears out of sight, and it becomes easy to believe that what we are seeing must be all there is to see.

All of this talk of perception reminds me of an infamous blooper by legendary snooker commentator 'Whispering' Ted Lowe, who produced one of the most memorable quotes in British sports history. At the time, not everyone with a TV watched in colour, and during a match, Ted uttered these timeless words, "Steve is going for the pink ball – and for those of you who are watching in black and white, the pink is next to the green."[2]

We understand this is funny because it completely misses its intended usefulness. But unless you're a comedian (or perhaps a politician), you'll rarely look to distract and confuse people on purpose.

Obviously, Lowe's gaffe gained notoriety because it was a one-off. He had demonstrated years of consistent clarity before that moment. But there is a lesson here. If we don't stop to wonder if what we're seeing is the complete picture, and forget to ask if others might be seeing things differently from us, the joke stops being funny. It becomes annoying. And in the end, we don't get picked.

Like a green tomato.

Through our tunnel vision, it seems for all the world that everyone else must be seeing the same one thing as us, and in exactly the same way.

Ian Morgan Cron tells a story of a children's eye hospital in his book *The Road Back To You*. The parents of children suffering from optical problems are made a special pair of glasses to mimic the vision of their child. Just as soon as those glasses settle on the bridge of their nose, frustration melts away and is flushed out by compassion, because finally, they see the world as their little girl or boy sees it.

The fact you can live with someone, and both of you see an entirely different world, is wonder inducing. Just a glimpse of what the other sees changes everything. Suddenly you are an alien, an explorer of parallel dimensions.

Take some time to wonder about the world as seen through the eyes of another.

This is a helpful practice to remember if (perish the thought) you were to get a bad review, or find yourself in a fight-to-the-death-tussle over artistic differences within a collaborative team. Try adopting a sense of wonder. Wonder what the other side is seeing that you're not. You might find the insight useful. Also, wonder what they're not seeing that you are. That, too, might help.

A whole other realm anticipates your arrival. A larger truth wants to emerge, and it sits waiting for you, resting on the edges of your vision, just on the other side of wonder.

Stealing Seed

Sometimes another person's idea or turn of phrase can be the catalyst you need to get you off and running.

Whenever I come across a thought I like, perhaps from a book or overheard in conversation, I make a note, usually intending to reiterate a similar point. But as I express the idea in my own words, often what comes out is tangential, and builds from the point I'd noted down rather than simply rehashing it.

Whenever you're stuck, try tracing someone else's idea, then lean into your intuition and trust your own inner voice. Eventually your own ideas will form and you will create your own distinct response to the initial thought rather than a direct copy of it.

This isn't cheating. This is planting a seed. And it isn't plagiarism because the seed never looks like the plant.

Don't flinch from starting with a seed you borrowed

from someone else. Just don't focus on emulating their every nuance, unless it is a practice exercise or you plan a career as an art forger. Instead, take that thought, idea, technique, phrase, or whatever has caught your attention, and take ownership of it. Plant the seed and see what grows, then incorporate the results into your work, where it will become something uniquely your own.

The idea is to incorporate a wide range of influences into your personal style, not become a copyist.

As Pablo Picasso is often quoted as saying, "Good artists copy, great artists steal."[1]

This is not unlike what British poet T. S. Eliot reputedly said: "Immature poets imitate; mature poets steal."[1]

Or for that matter, Russian composer and pianist Igor Stravinsky: "Lesser artists borrow, great artists steal."[1]

The deeper you look, the more names surface as having said similar things: Lionel Trilling, William Faulkner, Steve Jobs.

However, it seems likely that the phrase originated in 1892 with W. H. Davenport Adams, in what appears to be the opposite sentiment, when in an article he wrote: "… great poets imitate and improve, whereas small ones steal and spoil."[1]

Blatantly, someone has been stealing from someone. Which happily makes our point.

And they're not the only ones at it.

Brian Zahnd's book *Beauty Will Save The World* gets its title courtesy of a line in Fyodor Dostoevsky's novel *The Idiot*. Although the two books are nothing alike, Zahnd grew something entirely new from one seminal phrase that caught his imagination.

Irish singer-songwriter Glen Hansard and Czech pianist and singer Markéta Irglová released an album under the band name *The Swell Season*, which they adopted from the title of one of Hansard's favourite novels, written by Josef Škvorecký.[2]

American band *Sixpence None The Richer* derived their name from the writings of C. S. Lewis.[3]

Look around. This kind of seed stealing is everywhere. Creativity always builds on the work of others, no matter how subliminally it happens. Everyone combines from multiple sources. Wilson Mizner was right when he quipped, "If you steal from one author it's plagiarism; if you steal from many, it's research."[4]

No one's artistic voice is entirely original. No one can create in a vacuum without influence or input. You can't live in isolation and create wonders out of nothing.

Being the observant reader that you are, it won't have escaped your attention that the title of this book, *Brave Art*, is a play on words around the epic historical fiction movie *Braveheart*. I got the idea while pondering how

Stephen Pressfield's *The War Of Art* elicits thoughts of the ancient military strategy manual *The Art Of War*, by Sun Tzu.

Pressfield's idea and play on words sparked my own. I wanted to evoke the same kind of thoughts on how creativity and courage intersect. The trick is not to copy the style or technique but to be directed into new ways of seeing and thinking.

Whoever your influences are, don't merely copy what they saw but learn to see how they see. Then you will be the next word in the conversation, not just the last one on repeat.

We all want to share original insights, but what if no one else has noticed the kind of things we've seen, and no one else is producing similar work? Might it be we are on the cutting edge, discovering new things, or are we entirely mistaken, and destined to look like fools?

And so arises the temptation to copy more directly or adjust our work to fit an already established pattern or paradigm.

We adopt another's voice as our own because it comes pre-approved, and we think it might help us swerve criticism or avoid the necessary inner reflective work it takes to discover what we really think. Like a generic white-label product, we stick our badge on top of the voice we've assumed, and pretend like it's our own.

Some struggle with their creative voice because they have been conditioned to speak only when spoken to, and choose to keep to the safety of the script they've been handed. Subsequently, when it comes to saying something with their art, they default to seeking permission, double-checking that they are allowed to say what they have to say.

For instance, if a child, who simply wants to share what they've seen and how they feel, says the wrong thing to an angry, drunken father or to an overbearingly prim mother desperate to keep up appearances, it may lead to punishment. Over time, the child learns to express themselves only to please others. And so, we learn right and wrong responses based on the reactions of people, which then become hard-wired into who we are and what we say. If we never exorcise those voices, they will tell us what to believe and how to act our entire lives.

Listen to yourself. Be aware of who you hear speaking.

Sometimes we echo the voice of another in everything we say or don't say… say… say…

More Than An Echo

I fired up my computer and began typing a new email.

A few words in, the application suggested an end to my sentence. Not content with correcting my spelling, it now seems that artificial intelligence wants to finish my sentences. The phrase it suggested wasn't exactly what I had in mind, but it would do. So I hit the tab key to accept. It was, after all, quicker and easier. Convenience trumped any need I had to be the author of all my thoughts, so I sent off a message bearing my name that claimed to contain my words but didn't. They were given to me. They weren't my own thoughts. They were ones I chose to accept. But it saved me time and energy, and surely that's a good thing.

Isn't it?

Well, not really.

Because the voices we need are the real ones.

There is much to say, and much still yet to be said. If it is true that art speaks, then it must by definition have a voice. Your work is your voice. And you invest your life into that work. So speak up.

Resist whatever says you can't, you shouldn't, or you're not allowed. Resist the resistance. Push back against that which is pushing you.

Brave artists are the ones who explore new places and say new things. The timid are the copyists who speak little but echoes.

Your voice is distinct and personally attributable. So is mine. A parent easily recognises their child's cry in a riotous playgroup. And you always recognise your favourite actors the moment they speak. In fact, voices are so distinct that there are people who make a living impersonating recognisable ones.

James Arnold Taylor is one such example. He is a voice actor paid to mimic other – usually famous – actors. He describes the work he does as being, "basically like a stunt person for famous people's voices."[1]

You will have almost certainly heard him on TV or film but probably never realised. He has played a plethora of household names including Obi-Wan Kenobi and Fred Flintstone, and at different times has stood in the gap for such luminaries as Ian McKellen, Johnny Depp, Michael J. Fox, and Ewan McGregor.

So, how is this a thing you might wonder? Well, during filmmaking, occasions arise when a line, or even a word, may need changing after filming concludes and the famous actor is no longer available; or perhaps a computer game spin-off needs dialogue from the characters. This is when a voice-double such as James is given the call. Not least because they are much more cost-effective.

The fact such a niche exists is testament to how everyone's voice is unique and recognisable. People know us by our voice as much as our face. And the same is true of our creative voice. This is why using it feels so personal, sometimes even intimate.

Whether we think of voice as being the literal physical result of speaking or as a metaphor for our work, it is the same vulnerable act, because it is the bringing forth of a thought, idea, or emotion we've held inside and are now letting out to share with the world in some way.

Often people say they can tell a guitar part I've played or a song I've mixed. And although usually meant as a compliment, it used to get me down because I wanted to play like Gary Moore and mix music like Michael Brauer. I wanted to sound like those I looked up to rather than be recognisably me, because it somehow seemed true that if I could emulate them, it would give me what they had. But what *they* had was what *they* had. I had something different entirely. This realisation is a necessary part of maturing and of embracing your creative voice as your own. I don't mean just mental assent, but the embodying of it, the acceptance and living out of its inescapable truth that you can't be anybody else but yourself.

Do you ever wish you were someone else? Too late. You're already you.

Your work, your life, is more than someone else's style or formula.

Your voice is more than an echo.

Echoes do have their uses, mind you. Bouncing another person's thoughts back to them to confirm they've been heard and understood is part of skilful communication. But if all you do is repeat what you've heard, and add nothing new to the conversation, you're not even *having* a conversation. It's more of a two-person monologue. Likewise, if while talking to others you merely parrot things you've been told, you are more of a gossip than a voice. Carry on this way and you'll eventually conclude that your original voice doesn't even matter, even though it does. Being an echo might teach you technique, and even alternate ways of thinking, but it can never reveal who you are or why you are here. You learn these things when you break the silence, connect with your heart, and speak.

Nobody need even hear you, but you must start to speak. How else will you discover what it is you've got to say? Not that it's easy. In an age that has replaced kindness, respect, and empathy with accusation, ridicule, and groupthink, many feel safer when hiding their true thoughts and feelings.

But you have creativity burning like a fire in your bones for a reason. You have uncommon perspective, tone, and touch. These combine to become your distinct voice, and you have that voice for a reason. To have such a voice as yours and to say nothing would be a tragic loss.

This is when daring comes into play, creating your heart's true work in the face of trepidation. Finding and owning your creative voice in this way, defying fear's ability to define you, is an act of great courage. Feeling fear doesn't mean you are weak. Rather, it is proof that you care. It says that you are aware of the risks but are considering going ahead anyway. And choosing to do the work despite all this is an act of extreme valour. This is brave art. And your choice of art form doesn't matter nearly as much as your willingness to speak through it.

What is it you want to say?

Be honest now – even if you can't articulate it in words, you can feel it, can't you? Sometimes you might experience such intensity that it manifests as an involuntary moan, or maybe a shout. It's not uncommon to double over and let out guttural groans of longing. You're far from the only one to experience this kind of thing. This is your creative spirit protesting. Like a caged animal, it wants out. It won't keep quiet. It can't.

Open the door and let it go. Choose your medium and

start something. Whether your most potent tool is a brush, pen, camera, knife, piano, mixing bowl, your body, your voice, or finger paints with a class full of children, it matters not.

Whatever it is, just pick it up and speak.

Rutting Stags

Like rutting stags, they face off, sizing each other up. Soon every available ounce of wit and guile will be thrust to the fore. The door clicks shut, and each takes their place.

The game begins.

It is client versus graphic designer as a new project briefing gets underway.

This is a familiar scenario to me as my early career was spent in graphic design, working for a series of British agencies. Despite the profession's often glamorous image, I assure you it had little to do with rich companies bankrolling creative types so that they could indulge themselves in lofty artistic projects.

I discovered it had a much nobler purpose.

The outsider may see this work as being a gift to the

artistically inclined, laden with exciting opportunities to make beautiful things for gushing clients; but as a career choice, graphic design will frustrate the egocentric individual who believes they are signing up for a kind of salaried self-expression.

Not to decry the need for self-expression, of course. We all need it. Working purely for your own enjoyment can be regenerating. Personal projects are an essential part of recreation for most creative professionals. Many of us have extra-curricular artistic outlets away from our day gig. If creative, therapeutic play relieves pressure and makes you a happier, more balanced person then the world is a better place for it, and that is something to be celebrated because, ultimately, it is not a selfish pursuit, even though you start out as the primary beneficiary. However, if your creative life stays exclusively about you, with ne'er a thought for anyone or anything else, my guess is that it will grow weird and stay small; and so will you. Introspective self-importance is the hallmark of an immature creative life.

Far from being self-serving, I discovered that graphic design was one of the caring professions. To accept the call is to offer the best of your abilities as a sacrifice in the service of others. Skills you've honed through thousands of hours of hidden practice are given as an offering to bring about connections between people in ways they could never achieve alone.

Initially, you're hired in recognition of your skill and your taste. But if you are hired again, it is usually for other reasons. You are hired again when you listen and truly hear, when you see beyond yourself and glimpse the world someone else inhabits. You are hired again when you show empathy toward another's pain, and stretch your imagination on their behalf while teaching them how they, too, can learn to dream. You are hired again after proving yourself trustworthy with important things that belong entirely to another; when you interpret them clearly, and effectively present them with a pleasing and suitably styled aesthetic.

You are hired again when you can make it clear, make it attractive, and make it work.

While a painter may invite us to experience the world through their eyes, a designer steps into the perspective of their client and their client's audience. They seek to understand both parties and then work on the best way to connect the two. Done well, this is not so much a life of artistic expression as it is of creative servitude. You choose to lay down your life. And your keyboard, and mouse. Here, the greatest source of fulfilment comes not from making the art you want to make, but from being a conduit of meaningful interactions and transactions between fellow human beings.

Project by project, client by client, the designer's role is to discover each undertaking's purpose and audience. Without this clarity, you are lost at sea; rudderless on an infinite ocean of indefinite possibilities.

This work demands a whole other mind- and skill-set than that of the creator who has dropped their anchor in the safe harbour of self-expression. Design agency life pulled me away from the gentle ripples of the shore, out into turbulent waters. It was volatile and sometimes even felt dangerous. But here I learned that if my creative work was only ever going to serve me, it would never reach its potential. This can be hard to grasp, especially when you're young and still trying to tilt and spin the world on your own axis. But of all the things you might choose to serve, the least profitable is your ego.

Throughout the years of agency work, I developed technical skills and the aesthetic sensibilities for combining type, colour, and imagery in elegant and effective ways. But my biggest lesson was one you can't learn from a Photoshop tutorial. It was the training of my wilful soul in letting go. Letting go of good work that wasn't quite right. Letting go of an idea I loved but that didn't fit; and the next, even better one. Letting go of the disasters. Letting go of celebrated successes. We must hold on to what is good and let go of the rest, and I'm not sure that anything other than experience can teach us when to hold on and when to let go.

I believe this is true for every form of art and approach to creative living. It just happened to be the graphic design studio was where this lesson hit home for me.

Anyway, back to our meeting of client and designer.

These usually begin with the client showing the designer a concept they've spent hours mocking up, usually in Microsoft Word or something even less appropriate. Esoteric fonts, indecipherable acronyms, and garish colours abound, based on personal, idiosyncratic tastes.

Truthfully, it is a bit of a monster.
But it's their baby.
Their baby monster.

And they are emotionally bonded, hopelessly attached. However, if the design professional is to serve this client well, they know the client must first be detached from their singular vision. They need to let go. And are likely to need help doing so; the tendrils have usually grown deep.

Time spent on a project is always an emotional investment. This is what makes the work hard to let go of. Sometimes this happens easily and naturally as the conversation progresses. Most times, though, it is a bit of a wrestle.

Far from being straightforward, the necessary separation process is more like rough-housing with my five-year-old daughter – here you join us mid-bout: to release the death-grip she has on my ear, I tickle under her arm. In response, she lifts her foot to push my head backwards, so I grab her ankle, but instantly her free hand is back on my ear (now glowing bright red), and she stretches it way beyond the bounds nature intended. The tussle can be painful and frustrating for me. But my girl needs this fight, she needs to test her strength and push against someone stronger. I am gentle enough to cause no harm but strong enough to ensure everything comes to a close with both parties feeling satisfied and without injury. Knowing that she isn't the most powerful person in her world makes her feel safe, not threatened. She wants to lean into that strength but will only let herself do so once she is convinced by it. So we fight.

Metaphorically, this is how many encounters between designer and client play out. Or any other kind of creator and critic, for that matter.

And this is how we can also be within ourselves. The internal war is fierce and unforgiving when we find ourselves as both maker and participant, especially when relinquishing work or ideas we've been fighting to hold on to.

Most people want to lean into the strength and experience available to them, but it must first be proven worthy. Hence the locking of horns. And commencement of battle.

For this approach to have a snowball's chance of working, be clear on the intended outcome before engaging. Otherwise, everyone risks being hurt, while you achieve nada. If your foundational aim is to communicate an idea with as much clarity as possible, do all you can to see through the eyes of your audience, and empathise with how they understand what they're seeing. It's what *they* see that counts. Not what you think they see. And least of all, what you see.

Remember, this isn't about winning or losing. It is a stress test for every avenue of thought so that nothing important is overlooked or dismissed out of hand. This is the furnace where the steel of trust is tempered.

Letting go can be a fight. And often it needs to be. Releasing work you've invested a portion of your life into is no trivial matter, not for anyone, and so acknowledging the gravity of such an event can be cathartic. It declares that you did not, as feared, waste your time but were engaged in a necessary part of the creative process. Even though it hurt.

It is hard to not feel pain whenever our ideas aren't taken up. Our clients hurt whenever we must dissuade them from the original expression of their ideas.

If you're ever asked to offer constructive criticism, always do so with kindness. Often people have lived with their single viewpoint for a long time and have become attached more deeply than seems reasonable. Kindness leads to us seeing alternate possibilities. Pointing the finger leads to the other entrenching themselves more deeply in their position, no matter how ill-advised it may be. Even when dealing with yourself, the truth spoken with kindness is the quickest way to a changed mind.

When taking the lead in any creative act, we must practice letting go, moment by moment, over and again. Empathy will get you a long way here, as will humility; be sure to check any hubris at the door. Do this and you will prevent passionate debates dissolving into all-out war. Dignities will remain intact and everyone will leave smiling, ideally with the same number of teeth they arrived with.

This manner of conflict has raged for aeons because everyone has taste, even if it's bad. And everyone has an opinion when it comes to aesthetics. For example, while few of us would express strong feelings to a mechanic about how to replace a car exhaust, we have no hesitation suggesting to a designer how to improve their work.

It seems we are more inclined to share our convictions whenever our personal take on beauty intersects our lives and agitates our emotions. Notice how you respond to the way colour and shape are used on a page, or melody and harmony within a song. These have the power to awaken sleeping souls because the human soul knows they matter. Whether in the guise of music, design, painting, or a beautifully lived life, art provokes us and insists we respond.

This is why art critics are a thing.

And exhaust critics aren't.

So whether your fight to let go is within yourself or with other people, are you willing to risk the deeper water when the tide rolls in and offers itself to you? Will you relinquish the superfluous, no matter how attached to it you've become? Will the bravery of your heart expand to allow other people to engage with your work? In letting go, you open up the way for those who follow.

It is within your power to unhook the rope from its moorings and allow the tide to take you out, away from the familiar safety of the shallows and out into the depths. You can't be simultaneously tethered and free. There's no rope long enough.

This choice is your own.

Will you let go?

Loving And Letting Go

What happens if you design the cover of a book before it has any words?

I decided to find out.

As I began work on *Brave Art*, rather than following convention, I flipped everything and took a backwards approach. So instead of the cover being the final flourish to a finished work, as tradition would prescribe, it became my focal point: the target at which to aim my writing. I launched my graphics software before touching any writing tools, and transformed the book idea from a mental concept into something I could see. Just as an architect creates a visual before a brick is laid, I opened Photoshop before Scrivener, and designed a cover before a word was typed.

And it worked.

This approach may be impractical if you have no design

experience, of course, or you are a writer whose work is a component part of a sequenced chain of publishing events. But even then, temporarily pretending the cover of another book is your own can fire your imagination and get you moving. We are to do whatever it takes, even if it means tricking ourselves into belief and corresponding action. Because, whatever your creative outlet, it is easy to feel satisfied and then stop once you've arrived at a concept that you find agreeable. Having an inventive idea alone isn't the goal – it is just the start point.

The thing is, to the mind of a creator, unseen reality is still reality, and art without corporeal form is no less real. It holds space in a corner of your psyche. It is alive. You feel it. An impression, a desire, a knowing, it is the ghost of an idea with a slew of accompanying emotions.

This was the condition I found myself in. I was ready to write and knew the gist of what I wanted to say. But to do so with clarity and confidence, I needed a more tangible vision. So I crafted a cover for this imaginary book of mine and set about writing whatever a book with such a look might have to say.

There is a kind of fakery that makes things more real.

Deliberate imagination is at the heart of the creative process itself, not just its final work. Make-believe can make you believe, and helps you believe for long enough to see the job through. This is the substance of hope and the essence of faith. You commit and go, believing.

As I wrote, and the arrows of self-doubt assailed me, I'd engage in yet more reverie and change the author's name on the cover to someone whose work I loved, and pretend as though this was their latest release. This helped me distance myself from the fear of being self-absorbed, absolving me from self-consciousness, and freeing me to wonder if this was a book I might buy and read, should I have stumbled across it.

In further illusory shenanigans, I also screen-grabbed a book retailer's website and superimposed my cover into the line-up. Whenever it felt like I'd never finish writing, I'd use this website facade to visualise the completed book on sale in the real world, out there helping real people.

This visual context also served as a handy reminder that a book cover has more work to do than just look pretty. To earn its keep, it must carry out two jobs, which at first glance seem contradictory: fitting in and standing out. The cover should be at home within its genre, yet distinctive enough to catch the eye of the ideal reader, convincing them to stop and investigate. Unfortunately, some books agitate and repel. Others calm and ease us into an experience lasting longer than we anticipated. The best convey a message so evocative that just a glance can awaken our desire to know what treasures are hidden within its pages. The aim is for the cover, content, and layout to converge into a coherent whole that is so compelling the right reader finds it hard to resist.

People judge books by their covers, regardless of the idiom that warns against it. I'm as guilty as anyone, despite lofty ideals to the contrary. And knowing the inevitability of strangers judging mine with a mere glance, I sought to encourage the jury to be as amenable as possible. With a book cover, the point is never personal artistic expression but to communicate the theme clearly, and thus attract the right reader. And as this book matured during the weeks of writing, it outgrew its original look. As standalone artwork, I felt it held its own against anything else on the shelves, but I became less convinced it was the right face for *this* book.

The lesson is to recognise when your original vision stops working. You must be honest and admit when it is failing, because sticking to it rigidly will turn inspiration into frustration. Irrespective of how much you fell in love at the outset, whatever you're working on is never the pinnacle of possibility, and by attaching to it as if it were, you might hinder yourself. New growth never happens while ever you are trapped by the shackles of your first thoughts. Old ideas must die for new ones to live. Otherwise, potential goes unrealised, and the seed remains a seed.

Even when time is at a premium, having a period away from the work will allow you to see it more objectively; as can the opinions of others. Asking a few capable friends or colleagues will give you this kind of detached opinion quickly. We get emotionally attached to our work, which is why a professional seeks out honest feedback and listens intently, even though it smarts like tearing off a plaster. Simply liking something doesn't make it fit for purpose, so always be prepared to either change the work or change its purpose. You'd be ill-advised to use a cover you like as the front of your book if no one but you rates it.

However, if you can't bear that brutal parting of the ways, there's nothing to stop you hanging it over your fireplace in a nice frame.

It's not that I don't empathise with everyone who suffers in this way, because I really do. It is painful starting again today when yesterday you thought you'd finished. But if you want to serve the work well, this pain is sometimes unavoidable.

So, now you know. The artwork that wraps these pages isn't the original. I left that one behind despite investing days of hard, focused effort into it because, in the end, it didn't quite work. Was it a waste of time? Not at all. That cover gave me something to write about and became the catalyst for transforming a vague concept into definite words. But as I didn't want to hamstring my own book, I found the courage to let it go and try something else.

I had started with a cover, but no words. Now I had words, but no cover.

Emotionally, it was a little frustrating, but you can't get a better grip on things without first letting go.

So while the kettle boiled, I archived the files and removed them from my work drive, then took a deep breath.

File > New Document.

Just My Type

Are you much of a party-goer?

I'm not. But when my first book, *The Creative Wound*, came out in 2019, we decided to hold a launch party to celebrate. Toward the end of the evening, giddy from the attention and signing of books, I spotted a designer friend holding a copy open in his hand. I backed off to a safe distance and watched as he methodically thumbed through it. His designerly glasses gave him an authoritative air as he flipped the pages with steady intent, appearing to scrutinise every jot and tittle.

I'll admit it, I got a bit nervous. Were my jots okay? What of my tittles? Were my tittles too little?

I sidled over, hoping to end my suffering.

What even is a tittle?

"Hi Mark."

"Hi Rick."

"Nice typesetting."

"Thanks Rick."

We keep it straightforward, Rick and I. His is still one of my favourite comments since the book released because I knew he understood the job the type was there to do, beyond merely stringing words together. And I know Rick would tell me if he thought it wasn't working.

He knows that typography is a bridge for communication, not just to prettify a sequence of words.

Communication demands more of us than just words. It's not only what we say that matters but how we say it. Words carry tone, as does their presentation. The way elements are positioned on a page affects whether a book is read or abandoned. And if these are incongruent and confusing then so is the message. This applies not only to speech and words in print, but to every creative endeavour; each consists of a message and a method, the success of which relies on the effective interplay of relationships.

So how is it done?

Space.

Take this page, for example. You'll notice that space exists between the letters, words, lines, and in relation to the paper's edges. If these are not in proper balance, you will experience an unspoken tension while reading. And although stoutly you read on, bubbling under the surface is a constant nagging for resolution to this unsettling lack of ease.

These are the books unlikely to be read to the end, and certainly not treasured. Instead, they get bundled into the next charity shop drop.

You see, the reader is never just a reader. First, they are a viewer. Objectively they know they're about to read pages of written words, but emotionally and subliminally they're interacting on an aesthetic level. The work will be engaged with in the author's absence. Just as this book is. You and I are having a conversation, although not an immediate one. I can't answer your questions directly, nor clarify your concerns. So, I at least do my best to remove every visual stumbling block I can. Which, in the case of books, predominantly comes down to the judicious balancing of typeface and space.

In music speak, jazz trumpeter Miles Davis explains it this way, "It's not the notes you play, it's the notes you don't play."[1]

The space between notes is like space on a page, or the gaps between lines of dialogue in a play. Each art form has its equivalent. Space lets us breathe, giving us a chance to absorb and appreciate what we've just witnessed before we move on.

Whenever you provide space, you demonstrate respect for your work and care for your reader, viewer, listener. Making room, bringing order and balance, is to offer a warm welcome into your creative world. Like when you tidy up before receiving guests. When things are in order, people feel at ease and ready to listen. They are more receptive to what the artist and their art have to say whenever they are comfortable, which can often be at the cost of your discomfort. Artists and creators must often be the cushion, and we earn our stripes through tough lessons.

Like learning to touch-type on a manual typewriter.

For those born after 1985, a typewriter was a kind of steampunk computer with an instant printout facility. I remember at school we had to prove we could touch-type on a typewriter before being allowed near one of those new-fangled computer things – the technology that changed everything.

Our collective understanding of, and relationship with, typography transformed dramatically with the advent of affordable computers and the desktop publishing revolution that began back in the 1980s. The limitation typewriters had, which also remains their charm, was their monospaced output, meaning that the horizontal space taken up by every letter was the same, no matter how wide the letter itself. Because the blocks that punched the letters onto the page were of equal width, thinner letters such as *i* had more space around them. So the practice developed of adding a double space following the full stop at the end of each sentence, which allowed the reader to see more clearly a new sentence was about to begin.

This practice has long since slipped into obscurity because of the widespread uptake of proportional letter spacing, a technology coincident with modern word processing software, where the spacing around each character adjusts to fit its individual width. Even so, I still sometimes receive text from clients that has double spacing after every full stop. It's a little thing, yes. Nothing search-and-replace can't fix.

But it's the little things that betray us.

A once requisite technique taught as standard practice now serves as a clear indicator you're from another era. This highlights our vital need for maintaining sharp skills and for keeping our domain knowledge current. Giving up old, ingrained patterns may be unavoidable if we want to stay relevant. However, we cannot give them up if we don't know the need exists or that things have changed.

So we must remain alert, curious, and teachable, or the world will move on and we'll be left behind wondering where everyone went. Dreaming on its own is not enough; we must be skilled technicians in our craft. Otherwise, our technique will slip, and along with it the vocabulary necessary for us to speak and be heard.

When engaging with any kind of creative work, most of us dislike having to make allowances for avoidable niggles, such as out of tune instruments or spelling mistakes. They are distracting. And although we'll never delight everyone, we should at least try to remove all the hindrances we can.

The hours invested in finding and eliminating such problems may go unseen and unacknowledged, but whoever engages with our art will feel the difference. We will draw people in, not push them away.

If you think this sounds like hard work, then you'd be right. This is why a work of art is called just that – a *work*. If you care, it takes hard work, and hard work is never easy.

But the results are worth it.

Creative, Sensitive & Misunderstood

Two friends sent me the same article one morning. It offered advice on how to best work with creative people, which they thought I'd appreciate, given who I am and what I do. And some aspects of it were okay, helpful even. But they were offset by a sentence that bugged me.

I tried to read and understand it from different angles, but I simply couldn't fathom any other way of interpreting what I'd read.

The frame within which the author presented his thoughts was that creative people usually have major insecurities and big egos.

Wow!

Aghast isn't too strong a word to how I felt reading that.

Perhaps he'd experienced an unfortunate series of relationships with unusually challenging people. That could have been the case.

But I have hundreds of creative friends and colleagues, and few of them fit either part of that description. And, at the risk of stating the obvious, ego and insecurity are not in any way exclusive to – or intrinsic traits of – somebody who happens to be good with a paintbrush, words, or on the piano.

While it is true that many creatives are sensitive individuals, sensitivity is not the same as insecurity, although the two are often confused.

Many who are exceptionally creative belong to the twenty per cent of the population recognised as Highly Sensitive People (HSPs). These are neurodivergent individuals whose brains happen to be physically wired differently to the majority. As a result, their nervous system tends to be more sensitive than average, and they experience deeper cognitive processing of external stimuli. Elaine N. Aron has a helpful book on the subject called *The Highly Sensitive Person.*

In my experience, the biggest egos and demonstrations of insecurity I've seen in twenty-five years in the creative industry have come from management and leadership – not at all from the creatives I've led, served under, and worked alongside. The lion's share are humble people who are quietly confident in their abilities. And many devote their lives (often alone and in their own time) to honing their skills so that other people, or their organisations and products, can be presented as attractively as possible. There is little self-serving ego involved in any of this, but rather an abundance of unseen and unacknowledged altruism and love.

Many of us feel deeply the importance and weight of our work, and we are acutely aware of how much it matters to those who commission us, as well as the impact it may have on the people who will engage with the finished piece. This is why we stand our ground and present our case. And sometimes even dig our heels in. But this isn't ego. This is caring, often way beyond the call of duty.

In one sense, it is entirely understandable if some creatives *do* develop self-doubt over time if people are being taught to see them as uptight egotists, and don't give them a chance to be known or offer them space to present their case.

Quite honestly, seeding the minds of leaders and influencers with the thought that the next creative you meet is likely to be some kind of prima donna with an inferiority complex is untrue and profoundly unfair.

It is certainly not how I'd appreciate being led.

Instead, why don't we do our best to draw out the gold from whoever we meet, and speak courage to them so they pursue with intensity and integrity their passion and their gift.

That's what I'll be aiming for.

Relationship

Creativity is relationship.

Notice how everything is built upon relationship. From joyously smooth to crazily dysfunctional.

The way you relate to your creativity is a relationship. How a client or customer, viewer, or listener engages with your work, again, is a relationship. And this conflates when, beyond the work, the participants relate to you as its creator, as well as interact with one another.

Relationship also underpins the structures of the things you create.

For instance, if you were to sit down at a piano and play the three notes C, E, and G, you will hear a positive-sounding C major chord. If you then move the E note down a semitone to E flat and play the three notes C, Eb, and G, you will hear the melancholic sound of a C minor chord. The relationship between the notes makes a dramatic difference to the mood.

The same is true of colour. Whether we choose to consider the oils of one of the masters, a supermarket rebrand, or the paint you used to redecorate your kitchen, the combination of colours is make-or-break. Their interplay, and subtle differences, really do matter. If you are tempted to think otherwise, try wearing the black trousers from one suit with the black jacket from another. How does that conspicuous mismatch of tints make you feel? Like a dissonant note in a jazz piece, the clash is jarring and soon has you begging for a resolution to the tension.

Even something as elementary as a smile is all about relationship. This simple interaction is based on the shape and repositioning of the features of your face. In fact, your entire human frame is made up of a series of relationships, as bone after bone connect, held together by sinews in flexible tension.

The word *art* itself implies this kind of relationship and interconnectedness. Art is when the pieces come together well and form a pleasing relationship. We can think of the word *art* as meaning well-fitted: a rightness of relationship between elements. When they combine harmoniously, things have a beautiful freedom about them. But when they don't fit together well, or they're under too much tension (or not enough), or they have restricted flexibility, it's a different story. It's like your art becomes arthritis (a word derived from Ancient Greek, that means 'in relation to the joint'. Note also that both start with the same three letters). This painful inflammatory condition affects the movement of interconnected joints in the body and can be symbolic of stiff, painful relationships of any kind, including the composition of your work. You know it is happening when, instead of releasing joy and liquid ease, the parts crunch and jar.

So, given that the success of any creative endeavour depends on how well elements relate, it surely follows that the artist needs to develop good relationship skills – especially as relationships are difficult and require courage to engage. If they are alive, then they are also messy and unpredictable. They fall in and out of balance, experience seasons, and some even transition whole eras.

Given that relationships are tough, and that creativity is fundamentally all about relationships, is it any wonder we hit walls?

Even so, the call for us as artists and creative people is to transition our work away from formula and into relationship. Here, heart attitude is everything. The cost is higher but so are the rewards. Relationships require bravery. Formulas require following steps one to ten.

Going on an occasional date is easy. But drinks and a movie are not representative of the whole of life, or indicative of a relationship's full potential; it is merely the part you do to discover if you want to commit more deeply and walk through life together. You will never reach this point if you are the perennial flirt who never commits.

You must be prepared for the rigours of a relationship if you want to progress in your creative life. And sometimes you say "I do" with no idea of how you will.

A devoted monogamous marriage is hard work. Here we bare our soul and deepest feelings. We are known and learn how to be vulnerable, or at least we do if we're doing it right. We can't help but show who we truly are and what we think and believe. This kind of long-term, focused commitment helps us mature. And this is exactly the kind of depth-focussed relationship we need to cultivate with our work if we are to grow creatively.

To truly mature as a creator, your work has to grow beyond self-indulgence and aesthetic titillation. If it is continually all about you and your feelings, then you are missing the big picture. Are you looking to care for others or protect your ego?

Photographer and filmmaker Sean Tucker writes, "No matter how great a painter, singer, writer, or filmmaker you are, you are fundamentally no better than anyone else, and this gift you have to give was meant to elevate others, not yourself."[1]

Take *The Boy, The Mole, The Fox and The Horse*, for example. This beautiful book of illustrated musings by British artist Charlie Mackesy has become a worldwide phenomenon. It bursts with kindness, wisdom, and warm humour; as Charlie's timeless illustrative style, which to me subtly echoes E. H. Shepard's original drawings for *Winnie The Pooh*, beckons you into a world that instantly feels like home.

People from all walks of life love Charlie's book. And you don't achieve that kind of universally human connection by only ever thinking about yourself.

Your work will never flourish if your relationship with it is entirely focused on propping up a fragile but determined ego. It will atrophy. A tragically one-sided relationship is not what your art needs from you. If you've met anyone with self-involved narcissistic leanings, then you'll know just how draining they are. We must learn to listen and develop empathy toward others, ourselves, and our craft.

The deeper any relationship goes, the less susceptible it is to the metrics of comparison. You can't measure relational depth by numbers. The higher you pile up attainments on a shallow foundation, the quicker and more drastic the collapse will be. Deep roots are the most stable.

Perhaps true success isn't about going higher and higher, but deeper and deeper.

Most people find that a handful of deeper relationships are more satisfying than a multitude of shallow ones. That's not to say we shouldn't know a lot of people or be part of a large scene or community. You absolutely can go large and go deep.

To explain, let me ask you a pertinently pert question: has your left elbow ever met your right butt cheek?

For those of us not professional contortionists, this has likely never happened. Yet how long have they been near neighbours, and essential parts of you? Isn't it weird they've been so close for decades yet have never met one another's acquaintance.

This goes some way to demonstrating how we can be part of a body of people, and work together with others, without ever relating directly. Which is good news if you have difficult people within your community, or you are, like me, an introvert and want to belong but know you do your best work alone. So although you and I may never get to meet, we are still essential parts of each other in some way. We are wired to thrive as part of a healthy community.

None of us can reach everywhere alone, as those of us who've tried to style our own hair or fix our own teeth know only too well. You cannot always see yourself or your work clearly enough. And sometimes you simply can't get into the right position.

Whether it be for an honest critique or to talk things through because you're feeling low, asking for help from a source you trust isn't failure, it's wisdom.

Sharing the truth of where you are at, and facing it together with a reliable ally, will bring clarity in the face of confusion. Like on those hoarder TV shows, where a homeowner has built up such clutter and filth it overwhelms them to the point of paralysis, this can be how our interior life feels when we get stuck.

Enter the clean-up squad, bringing with them a huge dose of comfort and hope. They're not overwhelmed by the situation because it isn't their mess, so their objectivity helps them see a path out of the plight.

Whenever there's pressure or trauma, whether intentionally inflicted or entirely accidental, the fallout inevitably brings with it a sense of shame. When words or actions pierce us, we create an inner dialogue that can be uncomfortable. But, by bringing our story, soul desires, and concerns into the presence of safe people, suddenly we are eased, as more hands than just our own lift the burden we were never meant to carry alone. Our dependable relationships bring new reserves of resilience. And we survive.

Picture a lioness out hunting on the African plains, crouching behind a sun-scorched tree trunk. She waits.

A herd of zebras approaches. They're not hard to see. Their camouflage seems somewhat lacking, the black and white stripes a beacon for predators against the dusty ochre plains. But, curiously, it works. That's because the zebras don't plan on hiding against their environment, but to blend in with one other. To survive, they hide within their crowd. There is strength in numbers and safety within the tribe. They know isolation is deadly.

Putting your work out into the world can make you feel like a lone zebra, vulnerable to attack. And especially when you're unsure about how your work will be received. It feels inevitable a huge rejection is coming and you are going to be left all alone.

To protect yourself, it is tempting to withdraw and isolate. Perhaps, you surmise, you can beat rejection to it by choosing aloneness preemptively rather than having it thrust upon you. But isolating makes it easier for you to be picked off. And please don't confuse it with solitude, because they are not the same thing. Isolation is often used as a punishment, and with good reason: being alone with nothing but your thoughts can be tormenting.

When a creator cultivates a healthy relationship with themselves and toward their work, they find it easier to be alone and yet not lonely. Many times I've been engaged with interesting and important work, and days have passed without me seeing another living soul, and I hardly noticed. A healthy soul improves your creative life, and, returning the favour, a thriving creative life enriches your soul. And ultimately, the world is a better place for it.

Isolation may be punishing, but you cannot easily punish a creator with solitude. Consider John Bunyan, for example. He wrote a literary classic, *The Pilgrim's Progress*, one of the best-selling books in history, while imprisoned in the county jail, separated from his wife and children. He turned enforced isolation into an opportunity for creative solitude.

Not to say it's easy. Every one of us needs picking up at times. We've all experienced devastating reviews, suffered crushing client feedback, or had gigs where you gave it your all and the crowd went mild. You have no control over how someone responds to your work. Sometimes you may never find out; other times, you wish you hadn't. We all know what it is to lose heart. Which is why we must choose courage, because *courage* – from the old French *corage* meaning 'of the heart'[2] – is the source of our deepest emotion and desire. It is the seat of our convictions and the place of our strength. Courage is contagious and good people follow it, especially when it is motivated by love.

The English word *encourage* is also rooted in an old French word, *encoragier*, which means to strengthen or hearten[3]. As we give and receive words of courage we will raise up a worldwide nation of creators from out of the wilderness. Our words and actions impart strength to the hearts of others. Be sure to tell the fellow creators and artisans you know the good that you see in them. Speak to their strengths. Remind them of what they've achieved. Tell them what you think they're capable of. In doing this we change the atmosphere we live in, and together we all inhale strength instead of weakness, and hope instead of despair. This strength of heart allows us to stare down fear and turn it into acts of brave creativity.

It takes bravery to acknowledge your potential. And accept your limitations.

We offer what we have with generosity, and humility, knowing that it won't be for everyone, but will be perfect for someone.

And so we have three choices: hubris, fear, or love. We can hanker for admiring glances as we flaunt ourselves like an overly proud peacock showing off his plumage; or don our invisibility cloak and disappear altogether; or we can offer strength and encouragement by sharing what we have, while being grateful to, and for, those who've shared their gift with us.

I don't know about you, but after finishing a particularly good book or podcast, I often catch myself speaking out loud a 'thank-you' to the people who've imparted much needed strength to me. Sometimes I'll send them an email to let them know their work makes a difference, and I'll do so not worrying about getting a reply. It's about building others up. And it makes sense to encourage those you're receiving good things from, especially if you'd like them to carry on their work.

Remember When

Just make a start, for goodness' sake. Write something, man.

I knew I had to write. Books like this are made up of words, and, other than the title, this book didn't have any.

As I sat on our comfortable cream sofa, I stared right through the blank page on my laptop. The cursor's rhythmic blinking mocked me as it metered the march of time, and despite its continual motion, none of it had been forward. In an attempt to infuse my soul with inspiration, I had walled myself in with books on creativity, and I ached to find that cherished state of flow – when ideas erupt from the wells of intuition, and words supernaturally align. But all I had was comfort, and too much of it. The whole set-up felt domesticated and tame, disconnected and fake. I needed to feel some push-back; a response to my call, something. But the anechoic chamber I'd made for myself reflected back nothing.

I needed to feel the day.

So I put my laptop down, slid open the glass doors and stepped into the garden. A deep quiet replaced the low hum of mains electricity I'd mistakenly thought to be silence. The undulations of the breeze gently massaged this bed of calm, and the only disruption was the lazy cooing of a wood pigeon who sat on the studio roof at the end of the garden. As I listened, I noticed her song would always start on an upbeat, a reminder that even the most familiar and uncelebrated parts of life offer their own signature beauty to those who are paying attention.

As the murmuring pigeon and the brush of the wind lulled me into a daydream, I resurfaced in another era. This middle-aged man was suddenly nine again. Particular sounds and sensations familiar to the boy had reconnected me to a time when I'd made art entirely for the joy of making it, long before I'd known the adult pressure of creating to provide for a family.

Perhaps you've had a comparable period in your own life, when all you knew of creative desire was its unassuming purit. This, for many, was during childhood. But over time, this desire can muddy up, like a photocopy of a photocopy of a photocopy, and as a result, your current work lacks definition. So, to regain the clarity of your long-forgotten blueprint, it is important to revisit your earliest creative motivations and feelings.

The ten quiet minutes I'd spent in the garden helped me remember some of mine, and when I returned to the laptop, the words flowed and this book was underway. The nostalgia I'd entertained in the garden had released me from creative block.

Now, you may be wondering how a bird's song and the lilting breeze had, within minutes, reignited my creativity. That's a fair question. The answer lies years back.

During school holidays I'd spend a lot of time on my grandparents' farmstead, nestled away in the Yorkshire countryside. Although only a short drive from home, it was a long way removed from the tough working-class town where I lived with my family, and I savoured those days of solace in the country.

Here I was allowed the time and space to experiment with art and music, and was blessed to have a grandma who was both a pianist and a painter. Whenever I visited, she'd give me free rein of her studio, which was a converted barn adjoining the farmhouse (itself home to an upright piano and pedal-powered pump organ).

I have fond memories of summer days roaming the grounds, lost in discovery. During the morning I might paint with watercolours, or maybe oils if I felt adventurous. Then, in the afternoon, I'd perhaps map out the notes on my guitar fretboard to those on the piano. Or experiment with sound combinations of the organ drawbars. I was free to explore whatever I found interesting.

One of my favourite treasures for discovery was an imposing wireless radio that sat like a general on the sideboard. Its large speaker, shielded by a red cloth grill, leaned back into a polished walnut housing. I'd power up the valves and twist the chunky cream dials to separate a clear signal from the static, and then eavesdrop on the exotic worlds and strange new music I'd find there. It seemed like magic to me.

Elsewhere in the farmhouse, five worn stone steps led down into the cellar. I had a real affection for the cast-iron typewriter that lurked there. I loved the satisfying clunk of the military-strength mechanism as it punched black ink through ribbon onto paper. It was here I first saw my words as type on a page. It gave them a gravitas I found captivating. I pondered on how books were made. Where did the words come from? Who typed them? Where was this all taking place? So many questions. There seemed to be a mystery behind everything tangible, as though its substance was ethereal before it was ever solid. And the search for answers only increased my longing to understand this mystery of beauty, a mystery that few seemed to be talking about.

Those early days hidden away in the countryside passed with no enforced agenda and no pressure for a finished product, just a growing romance with creativity – and one that was always accompanied by the sound of cooing pigeons carried on the breath of the wind.

That era is now consigned to history, of course. Grandma

has long since passed, and the old farmhouse has new owners who have changed it beyond recognition. The studio now only exists in the memory of a few. Yet, despite the passage of over thirty years, whenever I hear a pigeon's song or leaves blowing in the tops of the trees, that old yearning returns.

And I know I've come home.

Nostalgia has its roots in two Greek words: *nostos*[1], which describes a returning home and *algos*[2] which means pain. The term originated in 1688 with the Swiss medic Johannes Hofer, when it was first observed in soldiers in the field, and thought to be a debilitating mental illness.[3]

Psychologists have since identified two distinct types of nostalgia: restorative and reflective. Restorative nostalgia is when someone tries to rebuild or recreate the past. Whereas reflective nostalgia acknowledges that the past has gone, and that we should focus instead on the emotional power those recollections provide us with today.[4]

I'm sure most of those Swiss soldiers longed for familiar sights, sounds, and people; and never for a bloody battlefield. Memories of better times can be crushing when our present reality is hell, but they can also be our proof that happier times are a possibility – and that this possibility is worth fighting for. The hope of returning home is a powerful motivator for us to endure and not back down.

Therefore, I suggest we make deliberate use of our creative heart's yearning to return home, and employ nostalgia as a galvanising call to arms against the internal enemies of our work. How we respond to this ache for bygone times, to feel familiar feelings again, decides our outcome. Don't wallow in 'how much better things were in the old days' because getting stuck in the past serves no one. It is pointless to wish we could go back. Not only is it impossible, but it amps up our frustration. But when deployed purposefully, nostalgia reminds us we have something worth fighting for, and instils in us a deep resolve to keep showing up. This is the hidden power it offers the courage-starved creator.

Nostalgia also makes us feel good because the act of reminiscing releases dopamine into our system, giving life an enchanting sense of romance and reward: a sepia-tinged escape from today's tedium. And happy feelings are more conducive to free-flowing and healthy creative work, even if circumstances are tough.

This idea is backed by solid research, too. After studying the effects that nostalgic thoughts had on writers, psychologists at Southampton University in the UK confirmed that reminiscing can boost creative thinking. Their study invited participants to complete a writing exercise, and those who brought to mind a memory of 'a sentimental longing or wistful affection for the past' before writing, wrote with more creative language than those who didn't.[5]

So, it turns out that rather than being an escapist's tactic for avoiding reality, having an ongoing relationship with our past can improve our future. Used as a reflection before taking action – like a glance in the rear-view mirror before putting our foot down – nostalgia is potent. Suddenly, our thinking is unlocked from the bounds of time or physical location, and thus offers our imagination a far bigger playground. It is an invitation into spaciousness.

This is reflective nostalgia, which implies a distance across time between our present situation and the memory we're reflecting upon. This sense of space encourages us to widen our thoughts and explore with a more expansive outlook.

These memories assure us of our lives' continued significance and that we belong, in both a physical and chronological sense. When we reminisce and notice just how much time has stretched out behind us, it also reveals just how narrow our current timeline position is. It's more fleeting than we think. Recalibrating with this perspective is vital for letting ourselves off the hook whenever it seems like we must produce perfect work and do so immediately.

This realisation also carries with it an assurance that more time is surely on its way, acting as a buffer against the fear of its scarcity.

So, by engaging in nostalgic thinking, we step outside of

time and space to experience our creative world from a timeless rather than temporal viewpoint.

Try using this technique whenever you're feeling claustrophobic or restricted. It is useful when you feel under time pressure, too, because it lifts you away from the clock and into an eternal space. And as artist and author Christ John Otto explains, "Eternity is not a lot of time, it is outside of time."[6]

If we start a project and are only aware of the present, we can feel as though the entire world is demanding we produce faultless work and produce it now. This pressure and mental claustrophobia only ever leads to performance anxiety and the shrinking of our creative capacity. It is in these moments that nostalgia restores vital calm by reframing our lives within the context of a larger story, and thus relieving us from the tyranny of the immediate.

Nostalgia helps us cherish the landmarks we've made throughout our creative journey, too. These are important because they are infused with rich personal meaning. Forget them, and our art loses its position in time and space, its purpose lost. Of course, it is dangerous to drive forwards if we're only ever looking backwards, but periodic reflection helps maintain our perspective, reminding us of who we are and the things we've already accomplished. These are so easy to forget.

It also helps to remember we are always in both a formative *and* realisation stage: we've arrived *and* we're still on the journey. For example, if we travel by train from Edinburgh to London we will stop at York. Although we've not finished the journey yet, we have arrived in York. We're a long way from Edinburgh but must bear witness to the fact we're now in an entirely new place.

We are who our previous, younger self has formed us to be; and we are also the substance from which the future artist will be moulded. As much as I might desire it, I can't go back to being eighteen again, lugging a guitar and amp onto buses and trains to band practice, but I can acknowledge it as one of the crucial eras that shaped who I am today. Our journeys take us through many such stages.

In *The Creative Wound,* I wrote about how Steve Vai's instrumental guitar album *Passion & Warfare* became the soundtrack to my writing sessions. Today, whenever I hear that album, it not only connects me with one of my musical influences but also to my first book. It reminds me of when I held a copy in my hands for the first time, and of the conversations that the book has sparked with readers around the world. These memories trigger feelings that fuel belief, because of the meaning that has been infused here. It reminds me of who I am.

Some days I need only hear the first few seconds of *Passion & Warfare* to remember that I have what it takes to write a book. I'm not trying to recreate the same experience, but the act of remembering emboldens me. And although I've written a book before, it wasn't *this* book. So I find the strength to write something new because I remember the last time, and I expect that more joy and connection with people is surely coming as a result.

So with one hand I grasp the familiar, and with the other, the new. I hold in tension the past and the future, and I create. This is the sweet alchemy of balancing confidence with the thrill of the unknown.

Your story will be different to mine, of course; and what works for you will differ, but the principle holds true: reflective nostalgia will draw out memory after memory, feeling after feeling, like an illusionist draws a row of handkerchiefs from up their sleeve. And this will help you rediscover the creative person you were in the beginning before any of the noise and distortion and fear ever happened. You – the innocent artist.

The Latin word for *innocence* means unwounded[7], which is how we all start out; and creative innocence is a state of being we're all aiming to recover and live from. This is a return to who we were before we learned to hesitate and second-guess ourselves, when everything we produced was alive and raw and uncompromised – when our hearts were daring and our art was brave.

What would it mean if you were to recover a life where that kind of innocence is again the place your work originates? What if the feelings of that time are still available inside you today and are a power source you can draw upon?

Gather a few objects to help you recollect those significant points from your journey. Ponder them, and pocket the treasures you discover, just like a child let loose in a sweet shop.

If you're stagnating or feeling under pressure, you have permission to end the struggle today. It's wearing you down.

Instead, retreat to a quiet place and bring to mind specific work you're proud of, or a creative experience that brought you joy. Recall those times. Relax into the memory.

Remember what it felt like when you were alive and artistically fulfilled. Be aware of the sensations in your body as they change to echo the memory. Then let the familiar, affirming emotions that arise ease you away from anxiety and into a state of flow.

This is who you are.

And it is vital you remember.

Take your time.

Then, when you are ready –

Go create.

Perfectly Safe

"Do all animals have chins, Daddy?"

My five-year-old daughter is an inquisitive and expressive soul. She questions, pushes boundaries, and tries unfamiliar things. I love that about her. Even so, I often have to stop myself from correcting her use of 'wrong' colours or for going outside the lines. I admit it, her rule breaking sometimes irritates me. My agitation seems built-in. I know experimentation and play are vital to every child's development, so why the pull to impose myself at the earliest sign of something I consider a mistake? Why are my 'right' methods more important than her curiosity? I have no need to prove I'm superior, so what gives?

Here is what my soul investigation uncovered: I don't want my little girl to be wrong. I don't want her to experience being found out. I don't want her to feel the pain of being weighed and found wanting. Therefore, I surmise, if I can show her all the ways to be 'right' perhaps she can avoid being 'wrong' – as if that's the key to a successful creative life: *whatever you do, don't ever be wrong.*

This seems true because from our earliest years we're taught how to think and behave, and woe betide us if we're caught in contravention. We must eat our greens or get no dessert; behave or Santa won't bring us a gift; and we should always colour within the lines. No, not that colour.

This narrative shapes our young lives, and adulthood does little to lessen it. In fact, it can compound, especially if we allow academia and bureaucracy to provide our only benchmarks for self-evaluation, because these often imply that all intelligent and ethical thinking is unavoidably dualistic.

If you perceive the glories of life as having to fit within a rigid binary framework you'll experience crushing pressure, low tolerance levels, and a growing internal fury. If you see everything as being either *left* or *right*, *black* or *white*, *pass* or *fail*, then whatever you do will have to be perfect, or be marked as a failure. And likewise, so will you.

Is it any wonder you baulk when showing up to create something new, artistic, or meaningful?

Embracing the unknown can present a paralysing dichotomy for creative people: if when you explore, you fear being intolerably wrong, then you'll crave control of the outcome before you even start. Yet the brave artist knows that original work demands uncertainty, not predictability. This can unsettle us. But, despite what our feelings may scream, is it as dangerous as it feels?

When creative people believe that feeling *uncertain* equates to being *unsafe,* canvases remain blank and songs unsung, the 'book in us' stays there and inventions lie undiscovered in garden sheds, covered in thick layers of neglect. Art and invention miss their moment because of how this disastrous miscalculation steals the spirit.

But confidence returns to those who discover that the greatest catalyst for creativity is uncertainty. Like a trapeze artist, we must dare to release our grip and reach for the next thing, soaring through the air with no idea how things will turn out. The thrill of this flight is the nature of creativity: anticipation of the next thing to grab hold of. Will you make it or will you fall?

If an outcome is definite before you begin, then what you're engaged with is not creativity. It is duplication. You might feel safe and secure, granted, but you're not creating. You are copying. And that is not the expressive life you always dreamed of. Surely?

Look closely enough and you'll find that every truly creative act is an act of bravery on some level. The more uncertain you feel, the more possibilities could be at hand. Uncertainty always comes bearing the gift of new potentialities.

So, what if you reframed your scared feelings as being excitement instead of fear? What opportunities might open up if you turned your "no" to a "yes"?

Perhaps what you need isn't to feel more safe, but to be more brave.

The more prescriptive we are during our creative process, the fewer alternate outcomes we allow. Exchanging future options for a feeling of security may seem like a good deal when our confidence is low, but in reality, this is a fool's bargain and entrapment for the unwary perfectionist. Under the premise of safety, our focus morphs from freedom of expression into control of outcome: in order to maintain our precarious equilibrium, we obsess over what we can manipulate, and how; policing people and circumstances alike in the hope we will feel a bit more sure of things as a result. But every move is tentative, second-guessed, and – ironically – uncertain. One mistake and this house of cards might topple, exposing our whole elaborate illusion.

Living this way, our mistakes never become openings for discovery or learning. Instead, each one is used as evidence against us by our accusers, those who examine our unhidden failings and judge us with irredeemable finality. And so we strive to keep our vulnerabilities hidden and exercise control over all that we can.

Even so, things still go wrong. No matter how many contingencies we put in place, no matter how hard we try, the unexpected happens and exposes our creative frailties.

Consider these examples:

A young woman commissions a photographer to shoot a portrait series. On seeing herself in the photos she responds with tears – and not the good kind.

A singer auditions for a choir and the choirmaster laughs, gleefully pointing out the weaknesses in their voice to the other singers present.

A graphic designer submits the wrong artwork to a newspaper and a weather forecast goes to print using dummy text. An inaccurate forecast is bad enough, but things get real when the local weather prediction for 22,000 people is a recipe for chicken chasseur. And the national outlook, a delicious vanilla pudding.

These are all things I've lived through. They're part of my history as a creative person. And I doubted myself every time and wondered whether I should quit and go do something else.

Ultimately, though, what our creative lives become isn't determined by what happens to us or even the mistakes we make, but by how we respond to the inevitable adversity we face. We cannot sidestep every problem or predict the unpredictable. Neither can we escape having flaws in our performance.

To create our life's true work, we must let go of these

unattainable ideals and grapple with the real world, and the real us. Brave artists don't skulk in the shadows, at least not for long. Instead, they march into the light, determined to see things as they are, even if the glare of truth causes them to squint. By acknowledging the demands of reality, they nurture the courage and poise to face it, not deny it. Creativity never happens independent of messy reality.

In the cult science-fiction film *The Matrix,* a faction seeks to free the human race from a simulated reality in which they are unknowingly trapped. Eventually, weary of the real world's brutal discomfort, one of the freedom fighters, Cypher, chooses to have his memory erased and be plugged back into the computer-generated construct. He happily abandons his autonomy for an illusion of ease.

Unlike Cypher, we don't have the technology to go back to the comfort our ignorance once allowed. And because we're committed to learning and growth, the temporary bliss of not knowing what we don't know is over. This is a good thing, because the realities we don't face up to and overcome will ultimately define our limits.

When you begin working with an art form new to you, it can be exhilarating. You're hopeful, excited, and full of energy. You're even having fun. It feels good. So much so that you keep working at it. And because you keep working at it, you improve. Eventually, as your competence level increases, you know enough to realise that you're not actually very impressive. And even though you've improved dramatically, your feelings insist that you're now worse than when you first began. You've moved forward, but it feels like you've regressed.

Stephen Pressfield might refer to this kind of thing as *resistance*. Seth Godin might call it *the dip*. St. John Of The Cross might say it is a *dark night of the soul*.

Whatever you call it, it is comforting to know that you're not the first to journey this way. Don't take it personally, because it isn't personal, even though we each face it individually. This is *your* journey. Nobody else can take it for you. And the only way is through.

You can see that you've progressed, although admittedly not as far as you want to, and you can't deny the gulf that exists between your potential and your current ability. Now is the time to choose whether to grow up or give up. And it isn't as obvious a choice as it might sound.

This moment is orientating, grounding. Finally, you know where you are. Before this moment, you wandered, and you played. But suddenly you're located. This is a healthy sign that you have put in the effort and are becoming conversant in your field.

It's just as Albert Einstein said, "The more I learn, the more I realise how much I don't know."[1]

So, feeling like an imposter can, in truth, be the most affirming sign that you're not one. Being unsure of your abilities is confirmation you are on the right path precisely because you are aware that you have room to improve. Just make sure you focus on your need to grow, not to perform perfectly – because perfectionism says you must do your thing without fault straight away, even though you never will.

Instead, focus on one area and work on making incremental improvements consistently and continually. Daily, little by little you'll improve. And perfectionism won't stall you.

Maybe you don't have to aim for perfection at all. Aim for excellence instead, which is to do your best with what you have and who you are right now. Nobody can ask more of you than that.

Oh, and if you are still wondering about this chapter's opening question, it turns out that only human beings have chins. Look it up.

Two Tyred

"Dangerously bald," they warned.

No, not my head, as true as that may be: my car's two front tyres. And for some reason, I couldn't settle on where to buy replacements. I don't have a regular supplier and usually plump for convenience. But the day was open-ended, and I had nowhere else to be, so no particular place seemed most convenient. There were no meetings or impending deadlines, so I could enjoy complete freedom of choice. And it took me an age to make one.

I wondered why. Evidently, there was something to discover here. So I dug in and let curiosity lead, rather than chiding myself over my indecision.

Each tyre centre was in a different location. Obvious, I know. What I discovered beyond this was that each location also had a potential storyline in my mind's eye. Each would make me feel different – different about myself and different about the world I found myself in. *Interesting, keep on looking.*

I also knew I wanted to use the time well and write some more of this book while I waited. (I'm writing this sentence in the fitter's waiting room).

It eventually dawned on me that my real concern wasn't about choosing tyres at all. I was agonising over choosing my story, the direction my life would take based on this decision. Suddenly, which tyre fitter I opted for had increased gravitas. Of course, I couldn't dictate every nuance of the narrative that would unfold. Far from it. But, my proximity to certain people and places could open up specific potentialities, and limit others.

This was the real criteria.

So, did I make the right choice? I don't suppose I'll know for sure. But at least I made one, and along with it penned the opening paragraph of my day. And consequently, some things happened. Maybe the best things. Who knows? But things certainly happened. The world is different because of this seemingly inconsequential choice of mine. My story is forever *this* because I bought new tyres on the outskirts rather than in the centre of town.

And my choice led me to affect another person's life.

As my car was being worked on, I stole an hour to pound away on my laptop and do some writing in a nearby coffee shop. As I wrote, a number of customers poured in all at once, and seating space shrank almost to zero. I looked up to see a gentleman of well-past retirement age fruitlessly hunting for a place to sit. I smiled, gestured to the empty seat opposite me, and he elected to join my world for a while. Had I not done so, he may have left and gone elsewhere. But instead, we shared a small space and a chat.

The curiosity that had led me thus far carried me on: what if that gentleman was feeling lonely? Cripplingly depressed, even. Perhaps our conversation had boosted him enough to face another day, lifted by the fact another human being noticed him and saw his struggle.

What if he'd been warmed by a simple invitation from a stranger to share a table?

What if today I had quite unwittingly saved a man's life?

What if I'd chosen to buy tyres in the city centre?

You see, it's not just the completed work that makes the difference, but the places you go and the people you meet because of the work.

Every part of your process contains the potential for a miracle. And you'll never see the major ones on TV, online, or in the press. The stories we're sold as the big stories are not the only stories. They're the smallest fraction.

Everyone has a story. In fact, everyone *is* a story. The question is, are we listening?

9485 Days Later

Here's a curious tale for you. It happened in May 2021, as I was writing the manuscript for this book.

Do you remember me sharing how I arrived at the title back in the *Stealing Seed* chapter? Well, there's more to tell, and I'd love to know what you think. More importantly, I'd love *you* to know what you think. Is the tale that follows just a curious coincidence or something more? You decide.

Here is what happened: on Wednesday, May 5, 2021, I wrote my explanation of how the *Brave Art* title originated; it being a play on words based on the 1995 epic film *Braveheart*.

The following day, Thursday, May 6, 2021, Jordan B. Peterson released an episode of his podcast, an interview with Randall Wallace, the screenwriter who penned *Braveheart*. Can you guess the title of the podcast episode? Of course it was. *Brave Art*.

Obviously I had to hear this episode and thoroughly enjoyed eavesdropping on the two-and-a-half-hour conversation. Here's where it gets even more curious. Toward the end, Randall Wallace mentioned his friendship with Stephen Pressfield. In the *Stealing Seed* chapter, I commented on how Stephen Pressfield's *The War Of Art* played a role in me arriving at *Brave Art* as my title.

I had no idea these two men were friends.

Somehow a book and film with no obvious connection to one another had worked together as creative catalysts for me, and now they had converged again, appearing together on this podcast episode, which also happened to bear an identical title to my book.

You have to admit that is a little strange. Don't you find it curious? I do.

What makes it even more implausible, at least to me, is the separation of all the components throughout time. I'm writing this in 2021. *The War Of Art* was released in 2012, a considerable 3403 days before the words I'd penned. And *Braveheart* appeared in 1995, a whopping 9485 days prior.

What is it that causes a book written in 2012 to combine with a film released in 1995 and appear during the same year within the work of two different people, who both decide upon the same title?

What does this all mean? Does it make you wonder? I'm sure it ought to. Perhaps it is evidence of the creative mind at play and a demonstration of the mystery of its working. It is spiritual as much as it is cerebral. Creativity is something you attune to and hear, not cause to happen by sheer force of thought.

How exactly did all that connect up inside me? Perhaps I'd previously heard of Wallace and Pressfield's friendship and forgotten. Perhaps Pressfield mentioned Wallace in *The War Of Art* and that knowledge is lurking in my brain's dusty cupboards, subconsciously guiding my creative connections without ever my conscious mind realising. I readily acknowledge there may be traceable reasons why I made a connection between the two. If so, it is no less amazing to me that we are capable of creatively joining dots in tangential ways without consciously realising it is happening.

Maybe it all took place in my subconscious. Maybe it was something in the air. (But what then constitutes 'the air'? And so opens a whole world worthy of our reverent wonderment). Although that does nothing to explain the timing.

The biggest wonder for me is the timing. Why would I choose to write about the process of how I arrived at my book title the day before Peterson's podcast released? And how could I know to plan such a coincidence? I'm not that clever. Not even subconsciously.

I'll be honest, if you'd asked me outright on May 4, 2021, I couldn't have even told you who Randall Wallace was. It wasn't until I researched *Braveheart* on May 5 that I discovered (or perhaps rediscovered) the man.

So, why on May 6 did a whole interview come out with Randall Wallace, bearing the same title as the book I was writing?

Had I been a day later I'd have missed the magic, and forfeited the enchantment. I might have been deflated, disappointed, and maybe even felt a bit of a fraud. I'd have missed the connecting of the dots that, at least for me, were signposts confirming I was travelling the right route.

Pay attention long enough and wonders become signs. They connect the physical and spiritual, pointing the way beyond the limits of logic as they disrupt the underpinnings of the linear mind with their intuitive directions.

I share this story to encourage you to investigate your hunches. Take note of the things that make you wonder. Lean into your intuition, not just rationale. I had dropped what I'd been working on to write that *War Of Art / Braveheart* piece and was rewarded with a mystical occurrence, reassuring me that I was working on the right thing, and at the right time.

Moments like these are our doorways into the miraculous: like Lucy stepping through the wardrobe to discover Narnia. Open the door. Put a foot in. Then the next. Walk through into the depths, beyond what you already know.

Are you not even slightly curious about what might be living on the other side?

Beyond the smooth, veneered surface of things lie mysteries and marvels that pass us by every day in our distractedness. Patterns, connections, relationships; they marry together outside the limits of time and space, and speak truths in supersedence of facts. And we miss them. All the time we miss them. We ignore their glory because we forget to be astonished. Nothing is truly ordinary and yet we live as though nothing is remarkable.

As G. K. Chesterton rightly put it, "We are perishing for want of wonder, not for want of wonders."[1]

I don't think most of us need more step-by-step guides on how to be creative. We would benefit more from simply paying greater attention and taking the time to wonder about all that we notice.

Attune to wonder.

Don't Die Of Exposure

I wonder how many bands are offered gigs on the promise of exposure?

Accepting too many of these is a quick way to kill a career (if they don't kill your sanity first). But accept them they do. Musicians turn up for free and play a fine show, hoping the spotlight will lead to them being discovered by an A&R rep who chanced upon them that night.

Of course, this scenario has happened occasionally. But in reality, the band are just being ripped off, undervaluing themselves to the point of, effectively, paying to play.

Consider the investment it takes to get artists worth hearing on to a stage – hours of personal practice, band rehearsal, cost of equipment, and travel expenses. Plus, people make personal sacrifices – holidays booked from work, time away from family and so on. How much does just one show cost in terms of money, time, sacrifice, and emotional energy? And they compensate all that with 'exposure'?

I'd like to say I'd never fallen foul of such scenarios, but, well, I can't. One day sticks in the memory, when I played twice in two different cities. I like to remember it as being akin to the summer of 1985, when Phil Collins flew first by helicopter, then Concorde, and finally another helicopter from London to Philadelphia so that he could play Live Aid at both sides of the Atlantic. But in reality, it was just me in a beat-up old MG full of guitars, pushing the speed limit so I could play at both ends of the M62. Same kind of idea. Just without the fancy air travel.

Anyway, up with the lark, I drove two hours down the motorway to the first venue – a prison, of all places – where I played and sang for over an hour, then had some great conversation with the residents for another hour. I then dashed three hours back the way I came and to the second gig. Here I played an entirely different set, this time ninety minutes on lead guitar for a band I was helping out. That day I'd left home at 7:30 a.m., driven 200 miles, given it my all – twice, and arrived home at 11 p.m. The cumulative remuneration for my efforts, as welcome as it was at the time, was a meal from McDonald's. It doesn't take an economist to tell you that you can't sustain a life that way.

My self-managed music career was making minimum wage look a cracking deal.

And it wasn't as if the music wasn't appreciated, either. Everyone put their name to glowing testimonials, invited me back, and recommended me to other people, venues, and organisations. But I'd made the mistake of not putting a monetary figure on my offering. I'd hoped this would be interpreted as humility and serve as an open invitation for the organisers to honour me with a commensurate gift. Apparently not.

Experiences like this taught me that, as artists, we must be the primary people to value what we do. We can't rely on anybody else to do this for us.

When it is doing its job, people lose themselves in their moment of engagement with your work. It becomes personal to them, transcendent, and transformative. And during that moment, nobody is thinking about the personal sacrifice it took for you to get where you are, sharing your art with them; and nor should they be.

You and your work are there for *them*.

But there has to be a point when its value is made clear, and an opportunity to financially support the work be made available. As uncomfortable as that may feel, without it you'll burn out, and so will your creativity.

It takes bravery to say you're worth something.

Provision

Imagine if they banned music, or films, or books. What if paintings were outlawed or dancing made a criminal offence? What would that do to our sanity, our hope? Every human soul longs to be affected in a meaningful way, and a regular dose of beauty and creative expression is vital to that. We need the healing and health that creativity, art, and beauty provide.

Despite this, some see the arts as nothing more than an expendable distraction for those who can't function in the 'real world', or an indulgence for people who are rich enough to not have to. But try taking away their streaming video, music, or digital book services, and see how long it is before the meltdown starts.

The thing is, if we get so much nourishment and entertainment from the creative community, why is it okay for so many of its members to suffer financially?

The challenge many artists face in the digital age is the expectation for their work to be impossibly cheap, or even free. The sense that the creative arts should be widely available, particularly on our digital devices, is producing a culture of one-dimensional, one-directional entitlement. We risk letting art become just another service, and the artist behind the art, practically invisible. Art, for many, is now digital content paid for with a small subscription to a big company, with the big company mistakenly seen as the creativity's source, too, instead of the artist.

Let's take music, for example. My wife and I were at a restaurant when a song on the sound system caught our attention. I asked the waiter who it was. "It's Spotify," he said; although to his credit he did go and find out the actual artist for us, not just the service it was being played on. (The song was *Parachute* by Chris Stapleton if you were wondering).

People who used to curate music with care are now happy to let computers choose it on their behalf. And if you don't happen to have a friendly waiter close by, you can download an app that will listen to whatever is playing and identify the song and artist for you. Undoubtedly clever as this is, it's not the same as when a person makes a judgment of taste and shares what they've discovered with others. It's digital, end-to-end.

Not that digitisation is evil, of course, because it isn't. But when the artist is reduced to being just a 'content provider', and is thus commodifying their art, problems arise because commodities tend to sell for as cheaply as possible. When I'm buying tea bags, all things being equal, I'll go for the lowest price. And who wants their work chosen just because it is the cheapest?

But art? Art has value, value that has the chance to appreciate. And maintaining this possibility is part of our fight.

I'm concerned that the shift in our collective perspective is taking us to a place where art isn't treasured as it once was. In times past, if we wanted access to the works that moved us, we had to hunt for them. We'd search for gems hidden in covert backstreet boutiques, or thumb through classifieds in niche publications for a lead.

Do you remember leaving a shop after investing in a well-researched, intentional purchase, clutching it tightly as you made your way home in gleeful anticipation? Do you remember swapping your discoveries with friends?

These feelings are the genuine treasures that art provides. It's not the creation itself, but its effect on us that gives it its value. Do you recall conversations and connections you made through sharing and experiencing that book you loved? That album? That film?

Focusing singularly on one particular work at a time makes for an intensified, deeper love. It's monogamous, committed, healthy, and stable.

This is the place true artists want to lead us back to, rescuing us from the scattered and shallow attention spans that the internet age has brought about. If we don't control our focus, we can become overwhelmed, flighty, and even anxious without realising. And deep, focused creative time is a remedy to this. Perhaps we should be leading the charge on demonstrating this as part of a healthier way of life.

The lifeblood of many big internet companies is continual new content, and we are the ones who provide it for them. If everybody was to stop posting, sharing, and uploading, their platforms would quickly become ghost towns.

That said, it's my conviction that as artists we ought to involve ourselves in the digital mainstream, while taking care not to become entirely dependent. In it, yes, but not of it. Like a restaurant owner who steps onto a crowded street to entice diners into his eatery, we should be present but not resident within the system. Temporarily step into it for one reason: to invite people away from the clamour of the crowds and into our own welcoming environment. Otherwise, the surging masses will carry us to a place we never intended to go.

We owe it to ourselves to be clear on what our work represents, as well as the things we will, and will not, subscribe to while finding our audience. In recent years the big tech companies and intermediary service providers have made some powerful tools available, which, used judiciously, can do wonders to increase our reach.

But we must never forget that these companies are all in business to make money. It's easy to sign up and pay up for reputable services, and yet make little progress. This is not to vilify any organisation, because making money is what businesses do; but how we relate to them is up to us.

They don't know us as individuals and are not benevolently trying to help us with our dreams, support our lives, or love our art. So it's our responsibility to educate ourselves and learn which tools are important for us, and how to use them well. None of them are magic bullets, and they require curiosity and patience to master. It's important we fashion our own strategic and tactical approaches, and see that we carry them out.

As artists, we must have our eyes open to what we sign up for, and be clear about what to expect in return for the investments we make. If you're in it for the long haul, picture your life ten years from now, and ask yourself if the decisions you're making today will serve you and the creative community well for the next decade.

Is what you're working on today in support of your art, or is it just 'content'? Do you dream of being a content provider or an artist? This is an important distinction to make. The answer to that question will inform how you engage with the online world.

It seems as though many creatives are pouring their

work into the funnel at the front end of the social media machines and have developed a kind of addictive co-dependency on these companies for their survival. The social media platforms need free, visually interesting content to keep going, they need to get eyeballs on to pages to sell advertising. And when artists see this as the only way of reaching a wider audience they keep on feeding the machine.

The disparity arises when many artists are only just surviving while some of the big tech companies gross more than entire countries.[1]

People form deep emotional connections with the art that has spoken to them or moved them in some way. You'll hear people say, "I love that song," or, "I love that book." Rarely do I hear anyone say, "I love digital media content." And when I say rarely, I mean never.

It is our choice how much we consent to our work being handled as a commodity. Because, if we treat our own work this way, we permit others to do the same.

The artist's job is to conceive of and build alternate possibilities and adventures, not produce more content for the social media machine. Any content you do produce should be to attract people into your world and to the real art you're making.

In just one generation, we've lost the adventure of tracking down elusive works of art and literature, and replaced it with a desperate need to dam the sensory deluge. Part of the artist's life now is convincing people to pay attention to something they've reached saturation point with, and are instinctively trying to turn off.

If they perceive us and our work as part of the noise, they'll tune us out. But if we invite them into an alternative world – a refuge away from the cacophony – then we have a chance.

The Full-Time Creative

I counted 567.

The next time you're watching a film, don't stop it when the credits begin to roll. Keep watching, and hit pause periodically to read every name aloud as they stream past. Take the time to appreciate that hundreds of people were involved in that single ninety-minute production. These are real people. Each one needs food, shelter, and healthcare, and some have a family to provide for. There are equivalents in every branch of the arts and creative sectors.

These are the unseen creators, the artists and artisans behind the work we are being conditioned to expect for pennies, as plummeting prices, the rise of digital-only products, and piracy, have disrupted, and in some areas decimated, the arts in recent decades.

Let's consider the music industry. For years, part of my

income has been from music, and I have friends in all strata of the genre. I know hobbyists, teachers, session players, house band musicians, studio engineers, and a handful of band members who are magazine-cover famous. And most, if not all, are reporting seismic shifts in what it means to earn a living in music today. For some, it has become untenable, and they are looking elsewhere to provide for themselves.

For instance, Rebecca is a singer who toured the world for years on exotic luxury cruises, and was a resident performer at a high-end casino five thousand miles away from home. In 2020, still in her early thirties, she took a job as a railway conductor, and now stamps tickets for a living.

Then there's Hannah, a world-class sax player, who has been making ends meet waiting tables and administering medical swab tests in her local town.

Another associate, an astonishingly good jazz pianist who gave his best years to professional music, now drives taxis. Most of his playing now happens at home, purely for his own pleasure.

Before Sarah and I were married with a family, I used to perform live, and in 2014 I released my album *Catapult*, which sold online and at gigs.

Since then there has been a dramatic shift away from buying CDs toward streaming music; from paying for ownership to paying for access. This has affected many artists' income-generating ability because of the notoriously low royalties that streaming generates.

For example, on June 30, 2018, the digital music distributor I use registered 11,234 streams of my song *Gold In These Hills*. Once the distributor and retailer had taken their cut, those streams landed me a whopping £12.08 in the bank.

Now, for simplicity's sake, let's imagine every one of those plays was by an individual fan, and in order to listen to *Gold In These Hills*, instead of streaming it, they had bought a physical copy of *Catapult* on CD for £10.

If we multiply £10 per unit by 11,234 individuals, we arrive at a much healthier sum of £112,340. Contrast that with the £12.08 I actually received for those plays and you'll see the kind of gulf that is appearing.

This is an oversimplification, of course, as I've not accounted for production or marketing costs, but it shows the kind of disparity between how we used to buy and sell music and what an independent musician must now do to survive making their art. I suspect it is easier to make money this way if you have a back catalogue and an established fan base. The streams clock up and money drops into your account because people already know you. But this is tough for the indie, especially one just starting out.

How do we get around this?

Consumers always have a choice as to where they spend their money. In the case of streaming music, we could encourage people to stop patronising algorithm-driven services, although most are unlikely to entertain what they see as a retrograde move. It would take significant motivation for them to jettison the convenience and low cost.

People need a more compelling proposition than the streamed-straight-to-your-pocket option so that we can convince them to spend money on art by dealing directly with artists, especially those within their own community.

The way society in general considers, creates, and consumes art has changed. And so to thrive as full-time creatives, we must shift our thinking if we are to understand the terrain and keep pace. Artists now have to be increasingly creative in how they make money as well as creative in making the work itself. You may be an artist, but you must also be much more than that. You're also a small business owner, and a lot of your time will be spent doing the things that make it possible to make your art: marketing, budgeting, networking, posting on social media, doing taxes, and so on.

It's a misleading notion to think you can sit and paint, write songs, or whatever all day long. That's not a lifestyle dream, it's a fantastical illusion, unless you are financially independent or your art is purely a hobby.

Being a full-time creative may require you to adopt a self-employed gig lifestyle. There are no company benefits, no annual leave, and no sick pay. You'll forgo the comfort of a monthly salary and embrace a continually unpredictable income. Depending on your field, you may be able to negotiate a monthly retainer, or garner regular support from patrons, or receive royalties. But these don't automatically happen. Which is why taking a creative passion beyond hobby status is not for everyone. This freedom carries with it extra responsibility, and it isn't for the fainthearted.

Perhaps you have dreams of casting off a day job and a boss. Just understand that if you do so, you must not only complete your creative work, but accept the additional role of replacing your old boss. This will require effective people skills, too, because, even if you are leading no one other than yourself, you must learn to lead yourself well, with strength, vision, and empathy.

Most people don't wonder what their boss is doing at the weekend. But you? You're not without a boss, you're now with one you can't get away from. You have a shower with yours every morning.

If you're one of the lucky few who has the proverbial 'big break' then grab it with both hands and enjoy it. But, please, don't put all your hope in that scenario bailing you out. This is a quick way to end up brokenhearted and disillusioned.

You'll need to be adaptable and brave if you want to engage the economic world of the modern creative and make money by making art on your own terms. But your honed imagination and curiosity will serve you well if you apply it to the whole of your career, not just your art.

It may be that you pursue multiple creative avenues and enjoy a portfolio career where one aspect dovetails into another. This has the benefit of you being able to rest from one thing while you focus on the next, allowing you to work full time while continually being refreshed. One popular approach is to mix your practice with teaching.

The point is, your skills and imaginative approaches are transferable and applicable beyond the canvas or stage.

And you will need them.

Work To A Budget & Budget To Work

If you depend on your creative wits to put food on the table, it is important to stay on top of your finances. Even if your art is solely a hobby, it will always generate attributable costs. As dull as it may sound, this is important if you want to live a successful creative life. And the cold, hard truth is that nobody is going to handle these business elements for you, at least not until you're proven and are already having a good deal of success.

If you find it unpleasant holding creativity and cash within the same thought, you're not alone. Creative people traditionally find it harder than most to talk about finances. And stereotypically, being a 'creative type' implies you are obligated to be penniless, as though hovering just above the poverty line gives you an extra sense of authenticity that having money would otherwise rob you of. So we struggle to know how to reconcile the relationship between art and commerce, especially when 'selling out' is held up as the unpardonable sin of the true artists' lore.

However, despite their celestial air and capacity to fascinate us with beautiful distractions conjured from nothing, artists also need to eat. They pay bills, provide for their families, and will one day retire. They are people. Professional creatives are not digital streaming services. They cannot be drained dry and expected to keep on producing. Being replenished is just as vital as learning your craft. Otherwise, you'll struggle to sustain anything over the long term.

It might seem taboo or uncouth for an artist to talk about money, but we must brave the discomfort of this conversation.

Most of us want to do more of what we love. We know there is more available than working a soul-sapping day job while squeezing-in some art on the side as a little passion project.

We've spent long enough merely existing, and want to experience connecting more with our true selves, investing our days into our life's work. We can't afford to spend any more time sleep-working the years away. But to enter the fray and create art that funds your life, that takes real bravery.

Perhaps we need to find different ways of selling our work. Many of my friends are full-time professional creatives and some have made a lot of money, but a lot live close to the poverty line. I'm not an economist by any stretch but can't help but wonder if there needs to be a new birth of the models in which we exchange the value of our art for value that supports the artist's physical life and wellbeing.

So I suggest you allow yourself time to work up to where you eventually want to be. Being patient and realistic isn't dismissing your dreams, it's giving yourself a chance. If you can't afford to live, neither can your art.

First, make sure your basic living expenses are covered. Next, investigate ways your art can pay for itself. Then, work on expanding your reach so that your art ultimately funds both itself and your life.

What if you choose to take a day job? Does that mean you've failed?

In short, no. Working a job can be the rest your mind needs so that when you return to your creative work, you are fresh and excited to get going.

But if a regular job with regular hours doesn't appeal, you could take on freelance gigs instead. Although this is less predictable financially, it offers you the flexibility of being able to plan your own calendar, and thus free up time for your own work.

Each context and scenario teaches you about yourself and helps you grow. Sometimes you learn that the dream you have isn't the dream you ultimately want. And often, experience is the only viable teacher of this lesson. So, getting that experience is vital.

Perhaps you could take a job that supplements and develops your current skills, and you consider it paid training. This savvy approach can be the perfect opportunity to avoid unnecessary debt, and to earn while you learn.

And there is nothing like working a proper job to instil in you a respect for the opportunities you are given, as well as a work ethic and people skills. The bonus here is that, rather than paying for all this education, you're the one getting paid. And even if it isn't much money, you are still gaining invaluable life and business skills, not to mention a portfolio of real-world work.

In my early design agency career, I would take an Apple Mac home on weekends to experiment and learn new techniques. A high-end professional computer and software were prohibitively expensive for me at that time, but thanks to my job, I had equipment available that others were paying a university to get shared access to.

During that same era, a friend ran a small recording studio just up the road from one of the agencies I worked for. So, while my workmates were spending their money down at the pub, I spent my lunchtimes holed away learning how to record and mix music.

Plus, I was at the head of the queue to learn the first digital camera the agency bought, back in 1996. And I was the first person to buy their own.

Do you see the pattern? People would say how talented I was, but honestly, I was never more gifted than anyone else – just more interested, and often more curious, focused, and hard-working.

As the great landscape artist J. M. W. Turner confessed, "The only secret I have got is damned hard work."[1]

The thing that people don't like about hard work is that it is hard work. It costs. Although there is a cost to everything. And a price. There is a cost to *not* learning, and a price for missing out on opportunities.

The good and bad news is that, through the power of our focus, we get to choose the costs and prices we eventually pay.

Choose well.

Embrace Restrictions

Every morning, Monday to Friday, TREE shows up in your inbox.

It takes less than a minute to read and gives you one positive, thought-provoking idea to get your brain pointing in a good direction.

You can join here: theforest.substack.com

I was asked to be a guest contributor by the owner, Jeff.

When he approached me, Jeff didn't ask if I would 'write something good'. Instead, we agreed on one subject (creativity), and a deadline. He then specified how many emails I should write and limited the number of words I could use.

This is restrictive, yes, but the trick is to view restrictions as your work's canvas. Creativity always requires boundaries – whether they be the edges of a painting, the three minutes of a pop song, or the 17 syllables of a Haiku – so embrace them.

Try this exercise: within the next 30 seconds, think of a brilliant idea.

Did you get one?

For most of us, the challenge is too vague, nebulous to the point of irritation.

Now try this: imagine you have a pencil and a teacup. Think of a way to lift the teacup off the table using the pencil.

The simple answer is to put the pencil through the handle and hold it at both ends, right?

Next, take the pencil and draw a picture.

Not easy is it?

But what if I asked you to draw a picture using only straight lines? You might come up with a house, or a skyline of tower blocks.

Much easier, isn't it? A specific puzzle is easier to solve than one without limitations. It may seem counter-intuitive, but to live creatively, restrictions are your friend.

So, what are your current limitations? What do these limitations make possible for you?

Constraints force us to think, to choose. And once we face up to that most sobering of all constraints – the inevitability that our life will one day end – we have a constant reminder that nothing can be realised except that it happens within boundaries.

What we are able to achieve is finite because we are physically finite beings. We dream, invent, design, build, and beautify better when we are fully conscious of our vulnerable frame and temporary physical nature. So if you want to live a creative and meaningful life, choose well with the time you have. Because you don't have all the time in the world.

This truth ought to urge us to become more resourceful and wake up to where we are and what we have.

We are here. And we have a lot.

Inspiration

If you stop breathing, you stop living.

Creativity is the same way. As breath is to the body, so inspiration is to the creative soul.

In order to create, we need inspiration.

It is easy to agree with that and yet also be unclear about what inspiration actually is, let alone how to get any. So let's define what it is and what it does.

Inspiration is the nucleus of every creative act and the harbinger of change. It empowers and enthuses the human spirit to live out its expression of goodness, truth, and beauty. Often arriving unannounced, and, on a good day, accompanied by an intoxicating euphoria, it brings with it exciting new ideas to explore. And if we capture these ideas, we can craft them into something tangible using the skills and talents we've nurtured. When acted upon, the natural result of inspiration is creation.

Inspiration illuminates darkened subjects. When under its influence, disparate concepts connect, ideas flow, and hidden things are revealed, never again to be unseen. Inspiration gives us our first glimpse of a new insight, such as the "Eureka!" moment attributed to Archimedes in ancient Greece after he realised the water he'd displaced in the bath must have been the same volume as his submerged body.

The root word for *inspiration* is the Latin *inspiratus*[1], which means to breathe or blow into, and the related Latin word *spiritus*[2], meaning breath, is where our term *spirit* originates. Breath and spirit have long been understood to be inseparable and indistinguishable from one other, synonymous with the act of creation and the essence of life itself. The ancient Hebrew word *ruach*[3] encapsulates this idea, too, translating as breath, wind, spirit, and life force.

Genesis, the Bible's book of beginnings, illustrates this concept well. Here, the creator breathes life into the nostrils of an inanimate clay figure, transforming the sculpture into a living soul. Having imparted the breath of inspiration into humankind, the divine then commissions this new life-form to invigorate the earth with exciting new people and vibrant culture. Whether you interpret this story as a historical account or poetic metaphor, the idea remains clear and its application consistent: every created thing has a story of origin, and it starts with an infilling.

When we're inspired, it is easy to find raw enthusiasm (a word that in ancient Greek meant 'to have God inside you')[4]. During these moments, our imagination lights up, invigorating our desire to create. This temporary lift is the kick-start we need at the outset if we want to turn imagination into reality. It affords us renewed strength with which to establish ourselves into a rhythm of dogged resilience until the work gets done. This burst of clarity and power propels us into action, fuelled by the desire to produce something significant with the opportunity we have been given.

And an intake of breath from a life-giving source is where it starts.

If we respond fully, we almost can't help ourselves.

Just as a fish is born to water, we are born into the atmosphere of inspiration. It is our natural air.

In.

Out.

Over and over again.

Without breath, there is no voice. Any singer or public speaker knows this only too well. The quality and efficacy of their voice is deeply rooted in how they control their breath. The same is true for all of us, at least metaphorically, irrespective of our genre. As creators, we each have a voice, the strength and clarity of which depends on the essence of what we first draw in. The tone, projection, and power of our output all depend on what we inhale. Be it air to our lungs, or influence to our souls, our immediate atmosphere becomes the oxygen for our expression.

You know that magical feeling at a concert, sports game, or theatre performance? Often we refer to that as being *the atmosphere*. We don't mean physical air, of course, but the combined emotional effect the people and place have on our soul.

As we interact, our collective presence produces a unique chemistry. Together, human beings create atmospheres, and these influence us. No doubt you have experienced the mood change in a room when a certain individual walks in. It causes a kind of shift in atmospheric pressure, the emotional equivalent of how the air is balanced inside a plane at altitude. It pressurises our internal world and affects the way we push against the outer. How we handle this kind of inner pressure affects the art we make, what we say through it, and, ultimately, if anyone catches its message. The lifestyle we adopt and the attitudes we learn contribute to the atmosphere we inhabit and the impact and influence we have on others.

I vividly remember the pungent smell of particular classmates who were regularly sent to school unwashed and in days-old dirty clothes. Even when out of view, we could tell when they were nearby. All we had to do was breathe. Their faces and names are still clear to me today, even though most of the other kids are now just hazy memories. And although the thought of old schoolmates not being adequately cared for saddens me, it serves as a powerful reminder that our presence can release an odour that people remember for years.

Some smells get on us. They stick. The same is true of ideas and attitudes. We readily absorb the essence of whatever surrounds us, soaking it in like dry sponges. Just as tobacco smoke clings to our clothes, the thoughts we embrace from the people, places, music, art, books, and media we surround ourselves with will either erode our creative vitality or reinvigorate it with new hope. Even if the ideas don't originate with us, if we stick around them long enough, they will become a part of us.

Answer these questions honestly:

What kind of atmosphere do you live in?

What are your habits?

What do you open yourself up to?

Who are your people?

If the place you find yourself has a bad smell about it, leave and find a better one; one with breathable air. Choose your atmosphere, upgrade your influences, and you will inevitably become more inspired.

For centuries now, artists have flocked to work in specific cities around the world for this reason. Creative hot spots have grown up in areas such as New York for fine art, Hollywood for film, and Nashville for music. Florence was a prime example during the Italian Renaissance that took place between the 14th and 17th centuries.

And while there are many pragmatic benefits for artists to make this kind of move, it happens for deeper reasons than financial expediency or market dictates. These factors are motivating, of course, but beyond motivation, the deeper reason is one of inspiration – breathing in the right atmosphere to breathe out the right kind of work.

It's worth noting here that *inspiration* and *motivation* are different things, despite the terms often being used interchangeably. A looming deadline may be motivating, for example, but far from inspiring. Motivation relies on external pressure to get results – the classic carrot and stick. This short-termism may work for a season but is ultimately dispiriting. The carrot leads to greed, and the stick to shame. Neither of which is conducive to us flourishing.

Conversely, inspiration is an inside job. It is an internally cultivated treasure hunt for beauty and life, not success measured by performance and affirmed by compliance. It is a heart-powered search for being and becoming.

Like-minded artists rarely relate to each other by offering rewards or meting out punishment. Instead, they remind one another of who they are and what they are capable of. Moreover, their presence alone often speaks so fiercely that, over time, words to this effect may even become superfluous.

As far as it depends on us, we must be intentional about the atmospheres we open up to. A polluted soul can develop over time without us even realising. But so can a healthy one. The empowering news here is that we get to choose the type of atmosphere we live in and how we respond to its influence upon us.

If you want to live a creative life over the long term, don't worry when you have nothing good to give out, that's the time to relax and take something good in. Reject anything that uses intimidation to coerce you into action, and breathe in the things that bring your soul alive.

The Day Before Everything

How far back can you remember?

To be honest, I'm not sure if my earliest memories are even my own. I suspect many are a composite of old photos and family folklore. It's hard to know for sure.

Do you remember being born?

It is rather ironic that the moment most parents will never forget is one the child can't remember.

We all arrived on the planet due, in part, to the seed of a man meeting the egg of a woman. And, even if the subsequent relationships have been wrought with shame, pain, and resentment, without them you would not be here. You'd not have seen the sky or the sea. You'd never have heard a bird sing or Beethoven's Fifth. You'd not have tasted ice cream or wept at a wedding.

Without parents, none of us would have experienced

one second of this astonishing, gloriously wild and beautiful planet we call home.

And yet, despite knowing this, none of us can recall our beginning, the moment we arrived. We're just here and, over time, slowly awaken to realise we exist. And the older we get, the more we recognise the 'hereness' of our being here. But even so, the moment of our arrival is ever a mystery.

By the time we grace the world with our appearance, everything is already in full swing, and has been for a long time. It is like joining a film part-way through.

G. K. Chesterton said, "With every step of our lives we enter into the middle of some story which we are certain to misunderstand."[1]

Missing the beginning of a story makes it difficult to make sense of the middle, but this is where we are. We bear witness to the place we find ourselves, and even become part of the ongoing narrative, but as for understanding the reason we're here or remembering our first breath – we draw a blank.

Our memory fails us, so we lean on eyewitnesses to fill in the gaps. They teach us who we are by recounting the tales of our life. And although we don't remember for ourselves, we instinctively resonate with this as being the truth.

It's sobering, though. Nobody remembers how they got

here. Nobody. And we all find ourselves vulnerable to the remembrance of others in establishing our history, place, and identity.

This is exactly where the art of our ancestors serves to guide us.

Tales told around the campfire, stories passed from parent to child through the generations, holy writings of the elders, ancient paintings, songs, and dances, all conspire to tell us who we are, where we came from, and of things that happened before we arrived.

The conclusions we draw here are the foundations upon which we build. They give meaning to our work, and context to our lives. Without this grounding we are lost and adrift in the world, yearning to create but never knowing why.

Origins fascinate the creative thinker. We are comfortable acknowledging that a moment of conception initiates all our work – we were there and saw it begin. Yet we have no personal witness to our own beginning, let alone the beginning of beginnings.

As the writer starts a new page, or the painter mounts a blank canvas, they witness the glorious moment of another new start. This moment of voidness echoes back to the artist all that they remember of their own personal beginning – nothing. And this haunts the creative mind.

Art calls us to contemplate the profound mystery of existence. Why is anything here at all? Why is all this happening?

Michaelangelo's masterpiece *The Creation Of Adam,* one of the world's most celebrated paintings, provokes such wondering. It's not merely its beauty or his masterful technique that grips us. It's the universal human question it poses about our existence and origins.

Art that is truly inspired invites us to consider these bigger questions. It is an invitation to hunt for meaning. To search, to question. And, sometimes, we discover unshakable answers with which we then lay a sure foundation on which to build our own work.

Creativity is both logical and mysterious, irrational and yet wholly reasonable. The creative act transcends the moment and reconnects us to the eternal, to the source of life and imagination, to a point of origin.

Home.

Treasure The Questions

We were on a family day out in the beautiful mountains of Snowdonia, close to our home in North Wales, when we happened upon a rock.

I know this isn't unusual when you're in the mountains, but this rock arrested my attention. There were plenty of other rocks to gape at, but no other reached out to me like this one did, protruding fiercely from the side of a mountain as if desperate to make contact. It was big, definite, sharp, and made of grey slate, typical of the region and its historical local quarries.

I wondered how long this rock had been there. Always? That seemed ridiculous. So I tried to picture the day it had arrived, and how exactly it found itself on the side of this mountain. It must have come from somewhere and arrived somehow.

So must everything else, for that matter.

Did it appear from nowhere, made from nothing? Did I? Once I wasn't, and then I was. As were all things, I suppose. But if everything wasn't and then was, that means everything came out of not anything. Which seems unlikely. The alternative must be, therefore, that there has always been something. And that something must not have had a beginning, because then that puts us back to all things having come from nought. Therefore, as far as my peanut brain gets it, either everything came out of nowhere and is made from nothing, or something eternal is behind all that we know.

I feel for my family. I honestly do. This is how I think. I can feel myself going. Sarah puts up with it all the time. As does that little girl of ours, sat chattering away in the back seat of the car, probably trying to block out my ramblings and reflections on this here rock. And she's another thing, that girl who is never out of my thoughts. I'm still baffled as to how, not many years ago, she didn't even exist. Although she didn't start from nothing exactly; there was an egg, and a seed, and a desire. But that rock, that didn't come about from an egg and a seed, did it?

Sorry. I'm at it again. This is what happens.

Anyway, that slate rock launched me on a mental excursion to the beginnings of the universe and back. The result being another bout of unresolvable internal chaos. I couldn't cognitively work it all out. But the pressure relented eventually as it dropped down from head to heart, from reasoning mind to intuition, before finally resting in desire – the desire to create. Be it a photo, a painting, a sketch, I suddenly wanted to capture the essence of the beauty of this thing, this rock, this profound mystery, and in so doing acknowledge my limited capacity to grasp its suchness, which stood as a representative of the whole of absolutely everything. Curiously, somehow, it seemed that painting it would help me be okay with all of that unknowing.

So, as I often do, I found myself trying to fathom an aspect of creation, its meaning, and its source, only to find that, at least to me, it was unfathomable. And again, my response was to create something of my own that had its own meaning, if only to me, and in so doing I, Mark Pierce, became a source of a thing. God-like, in the way playing King Lear makes you king-like. Having tried and failed to comprehend *every*thing, my instinctive response is always to make my own *some*thing. My small creative act being a microcosmic mirroring of the mystery I seek to resolve. Perhaps this ceaseless pursuit of mine is to see if I can better understand the nature of the eternal that lies behind it all.

It's when I hit this place of desire that I let go of my mental strivings, and at last, lean back into the spirit, and somehow avoid implosion. Instead, I am propelled into wonder and compelled to create.

One of the most-loved authors of all time, J. R. R. Tolkien said it this way, "We make … because we are made: and not only made, but made in the image and likeness of a maker."[1]

I find it comforting that creative minds far greater than my own share this reverence toward the mystery we all find ourselves part of, and the fact every creative act reflects its creator.

Erwin McManus succinctly attests to the same idea in *The Artisan Soul* when he says we are all "A work of art and an artist at work."[2]

You and I are both product and process. Object and verb.

Similarly, we use the word *creation* to mean both the act and the result. For example, by making a vase you engage in the *act* of creation, and the vase itself *is* a creation.

As human beings, we are artists and we are art. We are made and we make. Creator and creation.

I've reflected on this idea since being young. Its scope is vast, and worthy of a lifetime's thought. I'm still working to grasp it although I'm no philosopher, theologian, or scientist. Instead, I just take note of the things I notice. And I've discovered it is okay to monitor life and create based on the things you learn. Ponder things.

Consider a kitchen chair, for example. Most of us would agree that someone must have designed it, and someone made it. It is a result of intelligent thought and purposeful craft. Its form and function speak that to us. Who would argue? A chair's very existence serves as proof that its creator must also exist. Therefore, by extension, I can't help but wonder if our infinitely more complex world, with its spectacular landscapes and diverse life forms, isn't also presenting us with the same kind of evidence.

To me, the world is a remarkable work of art and a masterful design, which strongly suggests an artist and a designer would be behind the work.

Art is evidence of an artist.

The way I see it, either everything came from nowhere and out of nothing, or everything came from somewhere and from something. The things I interpret as being strong evidence of design, purpose, and intentionality always lead me to a theistic worldview. Or else the world and everything in it, including us and our creative efforts, must be entirely by chance and wholly pointless. Which I really don't like the sound of, nor believe.

You may see it differently. But this is me.

If you find it hard to grasp the enormity of the profound miracle that is our existence, and struggle to comprehend the mechanics and actuality of the world we inhabit, don't worry. You are not alone.

It is complex, wonder-inducing, and a big reason for letting yourself off the hook whenever you find creative work confusing or unpredictable. The notion of creation itself is mesmerising. The further down the rabbit hole you go, the more enigmatic it gets.

So, when it comes to your work, don't expect the process of your creativity to be any less mysterious. This is its nature. And this is its joy.

It is beyond my ability to figure out how, one way or another, the world and the life we all share came into being. I'd like to know for sure how it happened. I can mentally assent to the theories, yes, but I can't pretend I comprehend them with unquestionable certainty. I can't even do that about my own life.

So instead, I choose reverence. I choose awe. I choose astonishment.

I know what I believe and what I am convinced of, but I can't show you a video of it happening. I don't pretend to know step by step how everything got here – I wasn't around at the time to see it. Besides, I'd be charging more for this book if I did!

And while I am willing to accept that others may understand these things, or at least understand them better than I do, I can't help wondering if we are never supposed to have absolute empirical proof. Maybe faith is more useful to us than certainty. Maybe we are supposed to just believe. It could be this is how we work best. I tend to think this is the case, because it keeps us humble, leaning into the heart, searching, discovering, and enjoying the thrill of each new revelation.

And so, even though conclusions vary wildly, I am grateful for everyone who investigates with the intention of sharing their discoveries and thoughts.

I am thankful for every writer, painter, singer, poet, scientist, theologian, teacher; every observer and note taker who lives honestly in honour of the questions.

Treasure the questions.

Our Working Worldview

Our convictions about the question of origin profoundly affect what we say through our work, and even the type of work we do. If an artist is convinced that all they have is eighty years on earth before the finality of their death, they are going to approach their work differently to the one who believes their spirit will carry on.

The worldview personal to each of us takes the form of a narrative, with our work flowing out of that. The story I live in has personal intentionality at its source, where love imparts life, and leads to manifold expressions of creativity and beauty. As a result of this, I seek to extend hope to people because I am convinced this hope exists.

I have a strong theistic worldview coupled with an insatiable thirst to discover the meaning behind everything I come across. Settling the origin question has released me into being able to experiment and explore more freely. From a position of being approved of, I'm no longer working to try and gain approval but am working from having received it.

Your art will take on an entirely different tone and focus than mine, though, if, to you, the world is accidental, random, and ultimately purposeless, and a place where the strongest or loudest always prevail.

But I'm not here to convince you to believe the same things I do. Rather, I hope that by peering through my lens, you'll better understand my approach, which, in turn, will help you determine and clarify your own.

You don't have to think like me, but you do have to think.

Can you be original without considering origins?

Is it possible to find meaning within your creative life if, to you, the whole of life has none?

I resonate with the author of *A Wrinkle in Time* Madeleine L'Engle when she says, "As I listen to the silence, I learn that my feelings about art and my feelings about the Creator of the Universe are inseparable."[1]

Your response to the question of the meaning of life and the beginning of things is entirely your own affair, of course. I'm simply encouraging you to explore it and not ignore it. Because, whether knowingly or not, you already create based upon that worldview, so it would benefit you to be aware of what your particular worldview is. You'll be bolder in your art when you do.

And your creative life will thank you.

Cracking The Chaos Code

What ought you do when all dissolves into chaos?

I take my lead from the words of Genesis 1:1, the Bible's famous first statement, "In the beginning, God created the heavens and the earth." In other words, the initial priority of the divine was to be actively creative.

First, create.

I am fascinated by how the writer goes on to describe the primaeval environment as being formless, void, empty, and dark. And that the only reasonable response to this looming chaos was to create. Derived from Ancient Greek, the word *chaos* implies a chasm or gaping void, a confusing and disorderly place. It reminds me of The Nothing in *NeverEnding Story,* the malevolent power that engulfs the world of Fantastica in its dark, brooding formlessness.

This is your story and mine. These desolate seasons of life

visit us all. None of us escape them. Which is why we must create. This is our invitation to bring order from chaos. This is hope.

As human beings, our fight in the world is fundamentally against chaos and disorder in its many forms. Every one of us, every day, faces the unpredictable, destructive degradation of life.

Have you ever noticed those old cars that sit abandoned for years in the corners of farmyards? Do any of them improve over time? No. Not one. Iron rusts, wood rots, and weeds grow. We know this as *entropy*, a process in which things inevitably decline into a state of disorder and death.

Through our choosing creativity as a way of life, our posture naturally becomes one of resisting entropy. Where deterioration sets in, we beautify and restore, because it is in our nature to make and to make old things new.

I'm sure this is why some of the most creative people have also had some of the most chaotic lives. To cope with affliction and trouble, they had to create. It was their only reasonable response.

Every act of creation is our rebellion against decay, in defiance of chaos.

The antithesis to chaos in Ancient Greek is *kosmos*[1], which contains the ideas of order, harmony, arrangement, placement, and composition. This is where we derive our words *cosmos*, *cosmopolitan,* and *cosmetics*.

This idea of *kosmos* from *chaos* says that for creation or re-creation to take place, there must first be a decline or state of disorder. Whether experienced internally or circumstantially, our response ought never be resignation, but a leaning into imagination and the power of creativity to push back against the destruction.

Chaos isn't our signal to collapse.

Chaos is our cue to create.

Wetwang

If I was to hazard a guess, I'd say you've probably never been to Wetwang.

I used to live minutes from this tiny East Yorkshire village with the funny name. It sits quietly aside a busy road and has a population of just a few hundred. Unless you're hankering after fish and chips from the famous village chippy, or want to pay your respects to the late former Mayor of Wetwang, British TV presenter Richard Whiteley, it is the kind of place you go *through*, not so much *to*.

And yet, Wetwang has forever been immortalised in one of the greatest works of fantasy fiction – *The Fellowship Of The Ring*, part one of Tolkien's *The Lord Of The Rings.*

Have you ever visited a place that inspired someone else? It can be eye-opening, often because the place is so unexpectedly plain. We might struggle to understand how inspiration could ever happen here given how unremarkable it appears. This is because the location itself is rarely the sole cause of the inspiration. Instead, it grows out of an individual's interaction with a place in a kind of chemical reaction.

Person, place, and period in time combine to create a unique impetus within the creator.

Despite J. R. R. Tolkien being among the most famous authors in English Literature, few seem aware he spent eighteen months in East Yorkshire during World War One.[1] The British Army sent him there to recover after contracting trench fever at the Western Front. This is likely how he came to encounter Wetwang and its Old English meaning 'wet field' or 'marsh', the perfect name for the swampland region he detailed in his book.

Even in the trenches of World War One, when you'd imagine focusing entirely on your survival was perfectly reasonable, Tolkien carried a notebook and pencil to document his ideas; and as he passed through hell, Middle-earth was conceived.

Choosing to create when you ought to be in survival mode will remind you *why* you must survive. As you war against the hardships of life, don't waste the experiences you're having.

It's a sobering thought, but had Tolkien not experienced the horror of war and resultant illness, *The Lord Of The Rings* would not have been the same book (In fact, there may have been no book at all). The miscellany of places he visited, dialects he heard, and experiences he endured must have all influenced the universe he formed.

World events, natural disasters, and the choices and impositions of others can land us in difficult places, often through no fault of our own. And suffering may well result, both individually and collectively. As tough as they are, some things are beyond our control. But how we respond is always our choice.

Acceptance is not the same as resignation.

What if we choose to create and innovate in the light of our hardships, not despite of them? Our responses to the pressures we're under could be the catalyst for something new and revolutionary.

In *The Fellowship Of The Ring*, the main protagonist, Frodo, wishes that the struggle he finds himself embroiled in was not taking place during his lifetime. After reminding Frodo that nobody gets to decide the times they are born into, his guide, Gandalf, presents him, and us, with the same pointed decision to make: "All we have to decide is what to do with the time that is given us."[2]

Your experience may have been different, but in early 2020, due to the onset of the COVID-19 pandemic, the time given to me suddenly became a premium resource.

Responsibilities and restrictions dictated that I couldn't spend as long on my work as I used to (although I got to play a lot more with my daughter – which was both precious and exhausting.)

I'd often want to write but couldn't carve out time, especially as people with new creative projects emerged, seeking my help. This intensity made for a remarkable period, and is indicative of where I think we are headed.

You see, I'm convinced we're on the cusp of a new Renaissance: a great revival of art, literature, and learning. A time when we abandon trivia and return to things that have real meaning.

This kind of thing has happened before, too.

As theatres closed their doors during the early 1600s to help stop The Bubonic Plague from spreading, an actor by the name of William Shakespeare was forced to abandon the stage. Instead, he wrote.

Embracing work related to his initial direction, he continued to progress. Shakespeare didn't throw in the towel, even when his passion and livelihood were entirely shut down. Instead, he explored a new path, one that would eventually lead him to the revelation of his true greatness. Faced with the obstacle of The Great Plague, he adjusted his approach and didn't allow himself to be derailed.

Consequently, some of his life's most influential work emerged during this time, a time marked by societal upheaval and widespread fear. Both *Macbeth* and *King Lear* were born during this period.[3]

Shakespeare wasn't the only one whose landmark works were penned during a time of plague, either. Consider Geoffrey Chaucer. He wrote *Canterbury Tales* while sheltering from rampant disease, and based the whole narrative on it, reflecting the impact the disease had as it rocked society to its core.

As creatives and artists, we bring interpretation and soul to the events in the world. Yes, governments establish laws and the media brings its reports, but it's down to the artist to bring interpretation. The artist expresses the impact all of this has on the human heart.

Will you develop into one of the creative, resilient individuals our reeling world desperately needs?

Our call right now is to make peace with those elements that are beyond our control, and adjust our approach so that we keep advancing.

When things don't go as we want them to, it is normal to feel frustrated and even experience deep pain. And just as grieving our losses and disappointments is important, so is not giving up in light of them. There are some things that we must stop trying to control when they are beyond our ability to do so. Letting go is not the same as giving up. Quite the reverse, as it happens.

Sitting around growing anxious will not help us. Neither will trying to control everything. What helps is exploring possibilities, creating options, chasing dreams, having fun, and making plans.

This is called creativity. It is something everybody is capable of, including you.

Maintaining hope is essential during difficult times. And our ability to imagine a better future is fundamental to us experiencing that hope.

So if you know that your imagination, attitude, or skills are not what they could be, this is your time to level up. Do the inner work. We can transform and grow because resistance will build strength if we push against it the right way.

We'd all love the success that being the best in any field brings, but are we willing to embrace and own the same manner of suffering it often takes? This is not an easy thing. Ask any woman who has brought a child into the world. The physical strain of carrying an ever-growing burden for months eventually culminates in the agony of that final push.

As she holds her bloodied child for the first time, sweat pouring down her face from hours of labour, will you dare compliment her on 'how talented' she is?

This isn't talent, it is guts. It's not natural ability, it is courage.

This is the beautiful mess that accompanies every new birth.

And this is the essence of what it means to enter a new Renaissance (French for rebirth). It is a state of being, not a period in time. It is who we are, not when we are.

At times you'll carry the work in your heart like it is a lead weight; you'll suffer pain, meet resistance, and it will probably end up very bloody.

Birthing new life is not for the faint of heart. But many of us are about to discover that we are more resilient and brilliant than we ever knew.

During times of significant change, the things that made sense yesterday can seem wildly out of touch with reality today. What used to work, now doesn't. And nobody thought to give us a guidebook.

When the lie of the land radically alters, your map becomes useless. The brave move now is to ditch the map and pick up a compass. A map shows you the prescribed route, whereas a compass points out the direction you're headed and leaves you to discover your own way.

As things shift and sway, you may have to become like a sailing ship defying a headwind. Rarely does the wind blow perfectly. Instead, a good skipper adjusts the sail to catch it. Even when facing an opposing wind, a boat can move forward – by tacking. This is when the boat zigzags at around 45 degrees in relation to the wind, heading first left, then right, over and again. And although the journey is longer, the zigs and zags don't matter if you keep sight of your goal and are making progress.

When presented with less than ideal conditions, we see the world through different eyes, often perceiving more clearly than before. When the obvious is suddenly made impossible, imagination becomes our beacon. Through its light we see beyond the self-evident, and we develop curiosity about what might happen if we combine our resources in new and novel ways.

Approaching familiar things in unusual ways is healthy. Even uninvited experiences can work for our benefit over the long haul. The crux is how we relate and what we create. And uncommon beauty can result from the moments we've felt the most unsafe.

At age 64, and well into a successful career, the artist J. M. W. Turner had himself strapped to the mast of a steamboat where he stayed for four hours in the middle of a chaotic snowstorm. After the event, he admitted he wasn't sure if he would live to tell the tale.

The result of this experience was one of his most celebrated paintings *Snow Storm – Steam Boat off a Harbour's Mouth*, which is a violent vortex of light, sea, and swirling snow clouds, in the centre of which a ship is battered by the elements.

This seascape isn't a product of Turner's imagination but of how he felt while being physically restrained, mercilessly lashed by the storm's fury, and fearing for his life – evidence that the aftermath of frightening experiences can result in landmark work.

So, as we continue to make brave choices, perhaps the beating we're taking from the storm we never asked for will work into us a new resilience.

The specific opposition we face as individuals is unique to us, and thus our responses must be unique. This is why we need *your* voice and *your* perspective. The real you is not generic. Neither is your work, which is why it offers so much to the right audience. Therefore I urge you, please don't hold it back. If you have something inside that's desperate to break out, let it fly.

Let's create something beautiful in bold opposition to despair and play our part in the coming rebirth of creativity. And perhaps, as we defy the storm's intimidation, we'll emerge to produce the greatest work of our lives.

The Commissioning

Our calling is to awaken the sleeping and compel the conscious to dream again.

As our fractured world changes at breakneck speed, my question for you is, *will your life become the masterpiece it has the potential to be?*

Are you willing for that?

There comes a time for you to step onto the stage and unveil your brilliance: the moment we need you to shine. You've seen too much, and you know too much to sit any longer in the shadows. No, you can't remove the prevailing darkness, but you can shine a torch. Your light is made for the darkness. So respond to that ache you have, that ache to create with courage and conviction; and finally give voice to your heart, and, in so doing, bring new light into the world.

Although you may feel scared at the thought, I urge you

to take your place and do the thing that burns within you to do. Because your only other option is not to. Which surely is no option at all. Don't let fear be the arbiter, because experiencing fear is unavoidable if you are to find your true courage.

Fear is a response. But courage, a decision. Knowing fear doesn't mean you lack bravery. And real bravery bears no resemblance to bravado, that delusional swagger that some parade in the stead of genuine courage. Being brave is to decide on your direction and start moving, one choice after the next.

Today we meet at a crossroads and you can travel one of two paths:

1. Create
2. Never try

You either join with those who create, or acquiesce to the will of those who destroy.

This choice is your own.

Whatever your vocation and your joy, I hope you choose to live with the touch of an artist and a warrior's grit, releasing imaginative works and beautiful moments out of the unaffected overflow of a good heart, one grounded in a life fully lived.

You can bring forth wonders from who you are and what you have.

So whatever you choose to do with the time between your opening gasp and your final sigh, I implore you to infuse it with beauty and do it with courage.

Make brave art.

Please Leave A Review

If you enjoyed this book, please consider leaving a review on your favourite book website. Even a couple of sentences can make a big difference.

Also, if you know someone who would enjoy the read, please remember to tell them about *Brave Art*.

Thank you,
Mark.

Notes

The Essence Of Art

1. The Creativity Crisis In America! (July 10, 2012 / By Dr. K. H. Kim)

www.creativitypost.com/education/yes_there_is_a_creativity_crisis [Accessed on Nov. 2021]

2. Merton, T. (1978). *No Man Is an Island*. Harcourt.

3. Martel, J. F. (2015) *Reclaiming Art in the Age of Artifice: A Treatise, Critique, and Call to Action*. Evolver Editions.

4. Medina, J. *Brain Rules: 12 Principles for Surviving and Thriving at Work, Home, and School*. Pear Press.

Born In A Barn

1. The Shambles. https://yorkcivictrust.co.uk/heritage/civic-trust-plaques/the-shambles/ [Accessed on Nov. 2021]

The Nature Of Beauty

1. USA Today wrapped its newspaper with a fake cover about 'hybrid babies' with antlers to advertise a new Netflix show. www.insider.com/usa-today-fake-cover-hybrid-babies-netflix-show-2021-6 [Accessed on Nov. 2021]

2. Scruton, R. (2011). *Beauty: A Very Short Introduction.* OUP Oxford.

3. Beauty Will Save the World. https://brianzahnd.com/2010/12/beauty-will-save-the-world/ [Accessed on Nov. 2021]

4. The 16,000 Artworks the Nazis Censored and Labeled "Degenerate Art": The Complete Historic Inventory Is Now Online. www.openculture.com/2018/05/the-16000-artworks-the-nazis-censored-and-labeled-degenerate-art.html [Accessed on Nov. 2021]

Proper Art Or Propaganda

1. L'Engle, M. (2016). *Walking on Water: Reflections on Faith and Art.* Convergent Books.

2. Tolstoy, L. (2013). *What Is Art?* Digireads.com Publishing.

Break The (Jelly) Mould

1. McManus, E. (2014). *The Artisan Soul: Crafting Your Life into a Work of Art.* HarperOne.

Soul Trader

1. https://www.theguardian.com/music/musicblog/2010/

may/27/robert-johnson-blues [Accessed on Nov. 2021]

There's Knowing And There's Knowing

1. Lamott, A. (2013). *Help, Thanks, Wow.* Hodder & Stoughton.

2. https://www.goodreads.com/quotes/422465-the-most-beautiful-thing-we-can-experience-is-the-mysterious [Accessed on Nov. 2021]

Seeing Red, I Think

1. https://www.goodreads.com/quotes/8157203-there-are-three-sides-to-every-story-your-side-my [Accessed on Nov. 2021]

2. http://news.bbc.co.uk/1/hi/entertainment/3629569.stm [Accessed on Nov. 2021]

Stealing Seed

1. Kleon, A. (2012) *Steal Like an Artist: 10 Things Nobody Told You About Being Creative.* Workman Publishing Company.

https://www.artsy.net/article/artsy-editorial-four-iconic-quotes-artists [Accessed on Nov. 2021]

https://quoteinvestigator.com/2013/03/06/artists-steal/ [Accessed on Nov. 2021]

2. https://www.discogs.com/artist/1291067-The-Swell-Season [Accessed on Nov. 2021]

3. https://www.discogs.com/artist/230500-Sixpence-

None-The-Richer [Accessed on Nov. 2021]

4. https://quoteinvestigator.com/2010/09/20/plagiarism/ [Accessed on Nov. 2021]

More Than An Echo

1. https://www.astonmics.com/EN/artist-details/james-arnold-taylor [Accessed on Nov. 2021]

Just My Type

1. https://www.nytimes.com/2019/10/02/arts/music/silence-classical-music.html [Accessed on Nov. 2021]

Relationship

1. Tucker, S. (2021). *The Meaning in the Making: The Why and How Behind Our Human Need to Create.* Rocky Nook.

2. https://www.collinsdictionary.com/dictionary/english/courage [Accessed on Nov. 2021]

3. https://www.collinsdictionary.com/dictionary/english/encourage [Accessed on Nov. 2021]

Remember When

1. https://www.collinsdictionary.com/dictionary/english/nostos [Accessed on Nov. 2021]

2. https://www.collinsdictionary.com/dictionary/english/algo [Accessed on Nov. 2021]

3. https://www.theatlantic.com/health/archive/2013/08/when-nostalgia-was-a-disease/278648 [Accessed on Mar. 2022]

4. https://www.psychologytoday.com/gb/blog/time-travelling-apollo/201606/the-two-faces-nostalgia [Accessed on Nov. 2021]

5. https://www.fastcompany.com/3046676/how-nostalgia-fuels-creativity [Accessed on Mar. 2022]

6. Otto, C. J. (2014) An Army Arising: *Why Artists are on the Frontline of the Next Move of God.* Belonging House Creative.

7. https://cac.org/entering-dark-wood-2016-06-13/ [Accessed on Nov. 2021]

Perfectly Safe

1. https://www.theguardian.com/books/2019/mar/08/albert-einstein-speaking-by-rj-gadney-review

9485 Days Later

1. https://www.goodreads.com/quotes/171864-we-are-perishing-for-want-of-wonder-not-for-want [Accessed on Nov. 2021]

Provision

1. https://www.businessinsider.com/25-giant-companies-that-earn-more-than-entire-countries-2018-7?r=US&IR=T [Accessed on Nov. 2021]

Work To A Budget & Budget To Work

1. https://www.newstatesman.com/culture/2016/07/portrait-artist-it-time-we-looked-turner-differently [Accessed on Nov. 2021]

Inspiration

1. https://www.merriam-webster.com/dictionary/inspiration [Accessed on Nov. 2021]

2. https://www.merriam-webster.com/dictionary/spiritus [Accessed on Nov. 2021]

3. https://www.christianity.com/wiki/christian-terms/what-is-the-meaning-of-the-hebrew-word-ruach.html [Accessed on Nov. 2021]

4. https://www.businessinsider.com/enthusiasm-the-spirit-of-god-within-2012-9 [Accessed on Nov. 2021]

The Day Before Everything

1. Eldredge, J. (2007). *Epic.* Thomas Nelson.

Treasure The Questions

1. Tolkein, J. R. R. (2009). *On Fairy Stories* essay within *Tree and Leaf.* HarperCollins.

2. McManus, E. R. (2015). *The Artisan Soul: Crafting Your Life Into a Work of Art.* San Francisco: HarperOne.

Our Working Worldview

1. L'Engle, M. (2016). *Walking On Water: Reflections on Faith and Art.* Convergent Books.

Cracking The Chaos Code

1. https://www.biblestudytools.com/lexicons/greek/nas/kosmos.html [Accessed on Nov. 2021]

Wetwang

1. The Tolkien Triangle. https://www.visiteastyorkshire.co.uk/blog/read/2020/09/the-tolkien-triangle-b30 [Accessed on Nov. 2021]

How East Yorkshire inspired the worlds of The Hobbit and Lord of the Rings. https://www.hulldailymail.co.uk/news/history/how-east-yorkshire-inspired-worlds-5720627 [Accessed on Nov. 2021]

2. Tolkein, J. R. R. (2009). *The Fellowship Of The Ring.* HarperCollins.

3. What Shakespeare Actually Wrote About the Plague. https://www.newyorker.com/culture/cultural-comment/what-shakespeare-actually-wrote-about-the-plague [Accessed on Nov. 2021]

Shakespeare in lockdown: did he write King Lear in plague quarantine? https://www.theguardian.com/stage/2020/mar/22/shakespeare-in-lockdown-did-he-write-king-lear-in-plague-quarantine [Accessed on Nov. 2021]

Bibliography

Bayles, D., & Orland, T. (2008). *Art & Fear: Observations on the Perils (and Rewards) of Artmaking.* Santa Cruz, CA: The Image Continuum.

Bayley, S. & Mavity, R. (2019) *How to Steal Fire: The Myths of Creativity Exposed, The Truths of Creativity Explained.* Bantam Press.

Bragg, M. (2017). *William Tyndale: A Very Brief History.* SPCK Publishing.

Brison, T. (2016). *The Creative's Curse: Find the Creative Confidence to Walk with Your Demons (The Successful Creative Series).* Independently Published.

Cron, I. M. (2016) *The Road Back to You.* IVP Books.

Deresiewicz, W. (2019). *The Death of the Artist: How Creators Are Struggling to Survive in the Age of Billionaires and Big Tech.* Macmillan Audio.

Eldredge, J. (2007). *Epic.* Thomas Nelson.

Godin, S. (2020). *The Practice: Shipping creative work.* Penguin Business.

Grange, P. (2021). *Fear Less: How to Win Your Way in Work and Life.* Vermilion.

Gungor, M. (2012). *The Crowd, the Critic, and the Muse: A Book for Creators.* Woodsley Press.

Hibberd, J. (2019). *The Imposter Cure: Escape the Mind-Trap of Imposter Syndrome.* Aster.

Teems, D. (2012). *Tyndale: The Man Who Gave God an English Voice.* Thomas Nelson.

Judkins, R. (2016). *The Art Of Creative Thinking: 89 Ways to See Things Differently.* New York: Perigee, an imprint of Penguin Random House LLC.

Kleon, A. (2012) *Steal Like an Artist: 10 Things Nobody Told You About Being Creative.* Workman Publishing Company.

Lamott, A. (2020). *Bird by Bird: Instructions on Writing and Life.* Canongate Canons.

L'Engle, M. (2016). *Walking on Water: Reflections on Faith and Art.* Convergent Books.

Lewis, C. S. (2020). *Till We Have Faces.* William Collins.

Mackesy, C. (2021). *The Boy, The Mole, The Fox and The Horse.* Ebury Press.

Martel, J. F. (2015) *Reclaiming Art in the Age of Artifice: A Treatise, Critique, and Call to Action.* Evolver Editions.

Medina, J. *Brain Rules: 12 Principles for Surviving and Thriving at Work, Home, and School.* Pear Press.

McManus, E. R. (2015). *The Artisan Soul: Crafting Your Life Into a Work of Art.* San Francisco: HarperOne.

Moran, J. (2018). *First You Write a Sentence: The Elements of Reading, Writing … and Life.* Viking.

Otto, C. J. (2013). *An Army Arising.* Belonging House Creative.

Peterson, A. (2019). *Adorning the Dark: Thoughts on Community, Calling, and the Mystery of Making.* Broadman & Holman Publishers.

Tolkein, J. R. R. (2009). *The Fellowship Of The Ring.* Harper Collins.

Tucker, S. (2021). *The Meaning in the Making: The Why and How Behind Our Human Need to Create.* Rocky Nook.

Scruton, R. (2011). *Beauty: A Very Short Introduction.* OUP Oxford.

Tolstoy, L. (2013). *What Is Art?* Digireads.com Publishing.

Tyrell, M. (2015). *The Sound of Healing: Unveiling the Phenomena of Wholetones.* Barton Publishing.

About The Author

A creative professional for over 25 years, Mark Pierce writes, makes music, designs things, and takes photos. He lives on the wild and beautiful North Wales coast with his wild and beautiful family.

You can read more of Mark's thoughts on the creative life, sample his work, and join the mailing list at www.revelator.co.uk

Acknowledgements

Eternal thanks go to:

My beautiful bride, Sarah. Co-creating a life with you is one of my greatest joys, not least because you always point us back to what matters most.

Apple of my eye, Kyla. I hope this book teaches you as much about imagination and creativity as you have me.

My family, who continue to support me year after year.

The friends who journeyed with me, read my words, helped me process thoughts, cheered me on, and offered the honest feedback I needed. Medals of honour go to Tim Hall, Lauren Sapala, Andy Mort, and Ben Trigg.

Excerpt From The Creative Wound

I ran into the garden and stood in anticipation, a plump seven-year-old yearning for a flicker of delight as I held up a drawing I'd just finished, only for my open heart to be decimated.

"Shut up, you fat bastard."

The adult whose care I was supposedly in stormed straight past without breaking stride. I ran upstairs, locked myself in the bathroom, and sobbed for an age. My artistic heart and self-worth were left gasping for air from the blow of that sentence—the inevitable right hook following years of tiresome jabs.

Those five words confirmed my suspicions: the disinterest and disdain toward me and my creativity were real, and the wraps were now completely off so I no longer needed to wonder.

This was the moment my relationship with creativity

changed, the point it finally tipped.

I had no name for it back then, but this is my clearest early memory of what I now refer to as a Creative Wound. This is the infliction of damage to the core of who we are as creators. It is an attack on our artistic identity, resulting in us believing that whatever we make is somehow tainted or invalid, because shame has convinced us there is something intrinsically tainted or invalid about ourselves. This is the older brother of the imposter syndrome. Self-doubt on steroids. It is rooted deeper, and seems more true, than plain uncertainty.

Rather than permitting us the joy of plunging into the ocean of our untapped potential, a Creative Wound restricts us to a life splashing around in the shallows. Yes, it is safer, but it lacks any of the exhilaration we truly long for in our art.

A Creative Wound has the power to delay our pursuits—sometimes for years—and it can even derail our lives completely. This may sound melodramatic, but really it's not. Anything that makes us feel ashamed of ourselves or our work can render us incapable of the self-expression we yearn for.

On that afternoon in March 1980, I had no idea a long career as a creative professional hung precariously in the balance, but, aged seven, I was already punch-drunk, emotionally spent, and felt as if giving up might be my best option. However, in that moment, my young self knew I *had* to push against the crushing; and so, as more assaults came, the more I pushed.

I pushed *hard*.

Today, I get to play, record and produce music; I shoot photos for album covers, magazine editorial features, and stylised imagery for interesting people and brands; I design album artwork and book covers; I consult on marketing and brand direction for small businesses, and I coach fellow creatives. Oh, and I write.

Had resignation got the better of me that day in 1980, and I'd failed to approach my life and work with gritty imagination, I'd never be doing all that I enjoy today. Some of it, maybe. But certainly not all of it.

I constantly meet gifted people who are unable to share the brilliance that lives inside them because they are fearful or in too much pain. I'm thankful I've avoided joining the many who've abandoned their art in exchange for apparent safety. I'm not famous, nor do I aspire to be, but I do get to make things that make a difference. I'm living the life of my own design, and so can you.

Whether success for you means forging a full-time career in the arts, or simply being able to enjoy exploring your imagination without the companionship of debilitating emotions, this book will instil creative courage in you. Through it, you will recover your creative confidence if you've lost it, or finally discover your creative heart if you're yet to determine where it lies.

CREATIVE DERAILMENT & RESTORATION

In what follows, I will define what Creative Wounds are, how they happen, and discover ways they have been derailing your artistic life. Then together we will investigate methods of solving the persistent problems they create and learn how to get free of their hindrance so you can spend your time making art instead of drifting along in frustration.

Some books promise a step-by-step formula to the secret of creative bliss. This isn't one of those. That whole 'painting-by-numbers' approach to art has never resonated with me. Consequently, I don't have prescriptive methods to my work, and I refuse to cheat you by fabricating any here. Instead, I am offering you insight into *a way*—a pointing of the compass and an exposition of the terrain. This will help you establish a posture of heart and clarity of mind with which to guide your creative life.

My aim is to put tools into your hands and ideas into your head so you can experience restored wholeness and confidence in relation to your creative world.

I write from first-hand experience gained from a long career as a professional multi-disciplined creative. During my time with a series of UK design and branding agencies, I would repeatedly find myself being the unofficial studio counsellor/coach. This was when I discovered I had a knack for pinpointing how an individual had become creatively stuck. I would then help them work through the necessary process so they could return to an enjoyable and productive creative flow.

There was no on-the-job guidance for doing this, so in my own time I devoured scores of books and courses, and trained myself so that I could help my friends and colleagues more effectively.

The same pattern continues to this day within my own business, which I started in 2005. Scores of my creative clients have first needed restoration and renewed courage before we could effectively work on their project with any real freedom. And helping people with this internal work is far more important to me than simply turning a quick profit. Plus, I've discovered this approach is more profitable in the long-term anyway, as I've suffered far fewer abandoned projects as a result. Artists who pursue wholeness tend to grow in confidence rather than quitting in a panic part way through.

Because I understand the crippling nature of Creative Wounds, and have healed from them many times over the years, I am able, with heartfelt empathy, to take stuck people by the hand and walk them through a journey of reclaiming their creativity. This is where the idea for this book came from and what forms its basis.

For over two decades, I have drawn from the streams of psychology and spirituality and stood alongside fellow creatives in the trenches of their personal and professional battles until they secured their individual victories. Beyond artmaking, much of my creative life and work has involved diving into the mud and blood of this invisible war zone to pull people out. Survival and restoration from the brutality of a Creative Wound is a real thing, and I want you to stay creatively alive. So I offer you my perspective and the best lessons I've learned so far, along with suggested approaches I've seen bring undeniable transformation.

THE AIMS OF THIS BOOK

This book is a manifesto for helping you reclaim your deepest expressive longings. It's a rallying cry to those who have suppressed, ignored, or covered-over their dream of being creatively fruitful, to not let that dream die on the vine—as what a travesty *that* would be.

If creativity and pain are synonymous to you, be assured you are not alone. Using the guidance in these pages you will be able to locate the specific moments in which you were wounded and knocked off course. You'll also gain valuable new insight into what your *real* beliefs are, and how to cultivate more of the good while eliminating the toxic ones that serve only to poison your creative life.

This book is divided into three parts. The first focuses on the importance and impact of your contribution and why your creative life matters.

The second part defines what a Creative Wound is and

explains how to locate the roots of your Creative Wounds.

The third part teaches you my most effective methods for changing course back onto your true creative path, bringing with it a dramatic transformation of your entire experience.

Each chapter revolves around a single resounding theme: it is entirely possible to overcome whatever is currently holding you back from doing your best creative work.

So if you'll dare to open the door a crack, and peep out from within the safe haven you and your creativity are hiding, I've got some good things to share with you.

It's time to heal your broken art.

An Empathetic Guide To Recovering Your Creative Soul.

Combining heartfelt personal stories with inspirational and practical insights, Mark Pierce demonstrates how we can overcome artistic anxiety, find renewed creative courage, and produce meaningful work that matters.

It's time to heal your broken art.

"Simple, powerful, and works like pure magic. I haven't read a book that shook me up this much since *The War of Art* by Steven Pressfield."
– *Lauren Sapala, author of Firefly Magic & The INFJ Writer*

"A soothing balm for your creative battle scars, this is a book for anyone who feels they have more to bring to the world but suffer doubt, feel ashamed, or wildly over-think their creativity."
– *Andy Mort, musician, writer, & host of The Gentle Rebel Podcast*

Printed in Great Britain
by Amazon